# FIRST THINGS

## Special Features



## Lessons

### Unit 1: First Days



### Unit 2: First Nation



### Unit 3: First Freedom

# Quarterly Quiz

*Use these questions as a pretest or as a review. The answers are on page iv of This Quarter in the Word.*

**Lesson 1**

1. Psalm 104 echoes the promise to Noah that ___ will never again cover the earth. *Psalm 104:6, 9*

2. The psalmist notes that when God sends out His Spirit, the earth is destroyed. T/F. *Psalm 104:30*

**Lesson 2**

1. God said that is was not good for Adam to be what? (alone, nagged, sleepy?) *Genesis 2:18*

2. God gave names to all of the animals of the earth after He created them. T/F. *Genesis 2:20*

**Lesson 3**

1. When confronted, whom did Adam blame for his sin? (Eve, the serpent, himself?) *Genesis 3:12*

2. God told Eve that her sorrow would be increased in _______. *Genesis 3:16*

**Lesson 4**

1. The token or sign of God's covenant with Noah was the _______. *Genesis 9:13*

2. What did God promise Noah? (great wealth, never again to destroy the world by flood, many children?) *Genesis 9:15*

**Lesson 5**

1. What building material did the people of Babel use? (stone, concrete, brick?) *Genesis 11:3*

2. Before the Tower of Babel, the people of the earth spoke a single language. T/F. *Genesis 11:6*

**Lesson 6**

1. Abram's home city was _______ of the Chaldees. *Genesis 15:7*

2. Abram's deep sleep by God also involved what? (darkness, moonlight, owls?) *Genesis 15:12*

**Lesson 7**

1. Sarah reacted with _________ when hearing that she would become pregnant. *Genesis 18:12*

2. Sarah's son was named Isaac by Abraham. T/F. *Genesis 21:3*

**Lesson 8**

1. Ishmael and Hagar escaped death when Abraham rescued them. T/F. *Genesis 21:17-19*

2. Ishmael became skilled as a what? (farmer, archer, builder?) *Genesis 21:20*

**Lesson 9**

1. Jacob dreamed of a ladder with __________ ascending and descending on it. *Genesis 28:12*

2. Jacob promised to give half of all his possessions to God. T/F. *Genesis 28:22*

**Lesson 10**

1. God called Moses to rescue His people from the land of _______. *Exodus 3:10*

2. Moses wanted to know what about the Lord? (His name, His location, His oath?) *Exodus 3:13*

**Lesson 11**

1. The feast to remember being saved from the plague of death was called _______. *Exodus 12:11*

2. The Hebrews protected their houses from the plague of death by burning incense in the doorways. T/F. *Exodus 12:13*

**Lesson 12**

1. What did the Lord use to part the Red Sea? (firestorm, earthquake, wind?) *Exodus 14:21*

2. The escape through the Red Sea occurred at night. T/F. *Exodus 14:21, 22, 24*

**Lesson 13**

1. What was the main structure of the tabernacle? (an earthen mound, a stone tower, a tent?) *Exodus 40:19*

2. When the tabernacle was finished, a cloud covered it, and it was filled with the _________ of the Lord. *Exodus 40:34*

# QUARTER AT A GLANCE

*by Douglas Redford*

IN RECENT YEARS, the theme of "man vs. ____" has been used to form the title of certain television shows. There's *Man vs. Wild,* where the main character pits himself against severe conditions to demonstrate how he can survive. Another is *Man vs. Food,* where the show's star exhibits a "talent" for consuming all kinds of food.

As we read the Bible, it may seem that the title *Man vs. God* would be fitting! Such conflict plays an important part in the lessons for this quarter, which examine God's creative work as described primarily in Genesis and Exodus, the first two books of the Old Testament.

## Genesis: God Uses Individuals

When God created the man and the woman in His image (lesson 2), He created them with great potential and with great responsibility. Sadly, however, we do not have to read far into Genesis until we see the "man vs. God" scenario arise (lesson 3). Yet even after Adam and Eve's disobedience, God announced His plan to reverse the curse of sin by means of the seed of the woman (Genesis 3:15). This is the first reference in Scripture to the coming of Jesus.

The Lord's response to "man vs. God" was to establish a relationship with those created in His image. In spite of man's continual failure to be faithful to God, God remained faithful in His intention to rebuild that relationship. We see this in God's covenant with Noah and his sons (lesson 4). Following the judgment rendered at Babel (lesson 5) came the call of Abram and the establishment of a covenant with him (lesson 6).

The remaining chapters of Genesis record how God worked to fulfill that covenant. This was not a smooth road by any means; the account sometimes reads like that of a highly dysfunctional family! The issue became not only "man vs. God" but "man/woman vs. man/woman." Conflicts arose —between Abram (Abraham) and Sarai (Sarah), between Isaac and Ishmael, between Jacob and Esau, etc. But the Lord was not deterred; He kept His covenant promise intact.

## Exodus: God Creates a Nation

In time, Abraham's descendants became the great nation that God had promised. That nation's enslavement set the stage for God's call of Moses and the people's deliverance (lesson 10). God established the Passover (lesson 11) as a means for His people to remember the event that marked their freedom. This deliverance was given a dramatic exclamation point at the Red Sea (lesson 12).

However, such freedom was not a license for God's people to live as they pleased. If they tried to do so, then the "man vs. God" conflict would present itself anew. To remind the Israelites where their allegiance lay, God provided the tabernacle. This was a visible symbol of His presence for the Israelites throughout their travel to the land of promise (lesson 13).

## God Himself Takes Action

Sadly, the rest of the Old Testament becomes an account of the never-ending "man vs. God" struggle. We know from the New Testament that institutions such as the Passover and the tabernacle were not able to address completely the "man vs. God" problem. They are part of the shadow that the Old Testament law represents (Hebrews 10:1).

> ***The Lord's response to "man vs. God" was to establish a relationship with those created in His image.***

Ultimately, God took definitive action to reverse sin's destruction by sending the seed of the woman (Jesus). His death as an atoning sacrifice provided the genuine remedy. Only when *Immanuel* ("God with us") came was the conflict of "man vs. God" completely addressed.

# Get the Setting

*by Lloyd M. Pelfrey*

As a new nation under God, Israel needed to know several things: the reasons for the journey to Canaan, the patriarchal roots of Israelite faith, and the power of God in creation. Moses wrote the book of Genesis to provide answers, beginning with this majestic statement: "In the beginning God created the heaven and the earth." How was that different from creation concepts held by other nations?

## Creation Accounts

About 100 years ago, it was popular to suggest that Genesis 1 and 2 were borrowed from a "Babylonian Genesis." This document was found in Nineveh, where it was part of the famous clay-tablet library of Ashurbanipal, who was king of Assyria from 668 to 627 BC.

The document is titled *Enuma Elish,* meaning "when on high." It does indeed feature parallels with the Genesis account of creation, but the contrasts are even more striking. The plot begins with the murder of Apsu, a male god representing fresh water. This caused his spouse Tiamat, a female deity representing salt water, to want to avenge his death. The great god Ea then selected Marduk, the god of Babylon, to fight Tiamat, and Marduk (depicted to the right) killed her. He then used the water to create Heaven and earth, and he used her blood to make humankind. This contrasts sharply with the dignified, majestic simplicity of Genesis!

The Egyptians, for their part, had a dozen or so creation stories, and we recall that Moses had been trained with "all the wisdom of the Egyptians" (Acts 7:22). In fact, each continent, nation, or people group had its own theory of how things came to be (cosmogony). They are consistent in that there were gods involved. The usual goal of such accounts is to honor the chief god of a geographic area. The methods of creation tend to exaggerate the ways that new life is observed in nature: through mating (often among the gods), the use of eggs, and vivid imaginations about each of these methods.

## Covenants

Moses also showed how God used covenants in promising Canaan to the descendants of the patriarchs. Genesis 6:18, where God said He would establish a covenant with Noah, features the Bible's first use of the word *covenant.* The word is then used several times in Genesis 9 when that covenant is established (lesson 4). Numerous accounts of a worldwide flood have been found among the tribes and territories of the earth. Most such accounts have one family that escaped the deluge in some kind of boat.

The word *covenant* has other backgrounds as well. Genesis 15:18 (lesson 6) uses the expression "made a covenant," and in Hebrew it is literally "cut a covenant." This figure of speech is based on the fact that it was customary to cut (sacrifice) animals when making a covenant. This is demonstrated in the clay tablets discovered at Mari (northeastern Syria), which describe a covenant ceremony of the early second millennium BC that used the foal of a donkey as the sacrificial animal.

When the people of a region heard the word *covenant,* they usually thought about treaties or agreements between individuals or nations. A conquered nation (the vassal) might be offered an agreement by the conqueror (the suzerain). The regular formula included a preamble, historical review, stipulations, and consequences for disobedience. The gods were often cited as witnesses. Copies were made, and memorial stones were sometimes erected.

*Creation* and *covenant* were important concepts in antiquity! Do you see how and why these concepts are still vital in the New Testament era?



Graphic: Dorling Kindersley RF / Thinkstock

| | | |
|---|---|---|
| Mon, Nov. 11 | **Called to Live in Freedom** | Galatians 5:13-21 |
| Tue, Nov. 12 | **Setting Apart the Firstborn** | Exodus 13:11-16 |
| Wed, Nov. 13 | **Guided by Pillars of Cloud and Fire** | Exodus 13:17-22 |
| Thu, Nov. 14 | **Pharaoh's Change of Heart** | Exodus 14:5-9 |
| Fri, Nov. 15 | **The Lord Will Fight for You** | Exodus 14:10-14 |
| Sat, Nov. 16 | **Guarded from the Approaching Enemy** | Exodus 14:15-20 |
| Sun, Nov. 17 | **The Lord Saved Israel That Day** | Exodus 14:21-30 |
| Mon, Nov. 18 | **Offering Our Possessions** | Exodus 35:4-9 |
| Tue, Nov. 19 | **Offering Our Skills** | Exodus 35:10-19 |
| Wed, Nov. 20 | **Stirred Hearts and Willing Spirits** | Exodus 35:20-29 |
| Thu, Nov. 21 | **Skills for Every Kind of Work** | Exodus 35:30-35 |
| Fri, Nov. 22 | **An Overabundance of Offerings** | Exodus 36:2-7 |
| Sat, Nov. 23 | **Blessing the Faithful Workers** | Exodus 39:32-43 |
| Sun, Nov. 24 | **God Affirms the Completed Work** | Exodus 40:16-30, 34, 38 |

### Answers to the Quarterly Quiz on page 2

**Lesson 1**—1. water. 2. false. **Lesson 2**—1. alone. 2. false. **Lesson 3**—1. Eve. 2. childbirth. **Lesson 4**—1. (rain)bow. 2. never again to destroy the world by flood. **Lesson 5**—1. brick. 2. true. **Lesson 6**—1. Ur. 2. darkness. **Lesson 7**—1. laughter. 2. true. **Lesson 8**—1. false. 2. archer. **Lesson 9**—1. angels. 2. false. **Lesson 10**—1. Egypt. 2. His name. **Lesson 11**—1. Passover. 2. false. **Lesson 12**—1. wind. 2. true. **Lesson 13**—1. a tent. 2. glory.



# This Quarter in the Word

| | | |
|---|---|---|
| Mon, Aug. 26 | **God Knows Our Every Need** | Matthew 6:25-34 |
| Tue, Aug. 27 | **The Greatness of the Creator** | Psalm 104:1-4 |
| Wed, Aug. 28 | **Nourishment for All Creatures** | Psalm 104:10-18 |
| Thu, Aug. 29 | **The Cycle of Days and Seasons** | Psalm 104:19-23 |
| Fri, Aug. 30 | **The Exalted God of Creation** | Psalm 97:1-9 |
| Sat, Aug. 31 | **Praise God, the Creator** | Psalm 104:31-35 |
| Sun, Sep. 1 | **God, Our Creator and Sustainer** | Psalm 104:5-9, 24-30 |
| Mon, Sep. 2 | **Living Creatures of Every Kind** | Genesis 1:20-25 |
| Tue, Sep. 3 | **Made in the Image of God** | Genesis 1:26-31 |
| Wed, Sep. 4 | **Formed from the Dust** | Genesis 2:1-9 |
| Thu, Sep. 5 | **In the Likeness of God** | Genesis 5:1-5 |
| Fri, Sep. 6 | **Made a Little Lower than God** | Psalm 8 |
| Sat, Sep. 7 | **Created in the Likeness of God** | Ephesians 4:17-24 |
| Sun, Sep. 8 | **Created Male and Female** | Genesis 2:18-25 |
| Mon, Sep. 9 | **Obeying God's Voice** | Exodus 19:3-8 |
| Tue, Sep. 10 | **The Blessing in Obedience** | Deuteronomy 11:26-32 |
| Wed, Sep. 11 | **Choosing the Life of Obedience** | Deuteronomy 30:11-20 |
| Thu, Sep. 12 | **Obeying God Above All** | Acts 5:27-42 |
| Fri, Sep. 13 | **The Enticement to Disobey** | Genesis 3:1-7 |
| Sat, Sep. 14 | **The Punishment for Disobedience** | Genesis 3:18-24 |
| Sun, Sep. 15 | **The Consequences of Disobedience** | Genesis 3:8-17 |

| | | |
|---|---|---|
| Mon, Sep. 16 | **An Invitation to Covenant with God** | Genesis 6:11-22 |
| Tue, Sep. 17 | **Doing All the Lord Commands** | Genesis 7:1-10 |
| Wed, Sep. 18 | **Preserved in the Ark** | Genesis 7:11-24 |
| Thu, Sep. 19 | **Waiting for the Waters to Subside** | Genesis 8:1-12 |
| Fri, Sep. 20 | **A Sacrifice Pleasing to God** | Genesis 8:13-22 |
| Sat, Sep. 21 | **God's Covenant with All Humanity** | Genesis 9:1-7 |
| Sun, Sep. 22 | **Remembering the Everlasting Covenant** | Genesis 9:8-17 |
| Mon, Sep. 23 | **Words Lacking Knowledge** | Job 38:1-7 |
| Tue, Sep. 24 | **Limited Understanding and Influence** | Job 38:12-18 |
| Wed, Sep. 25 | **The Expanse Beyond Human Control** | Job 38:28-38 |
| Thu, Sep. 26 | **Overshadowed by God's Greatness** | Job 40:6-14 |
| Fri, Sep. 27 | **The Wrath of the Lord** | 2 Chronicles 34:14-21 |
| Sat, Sep. 28 | **A Humble and Penitent Heart** | 2 Chronicles 34:22-28 |
| Sun, Sep. 29 | **Human Achievement Without God** | Genesis 11:1-9 |
| Mon, Sep. 30 | **The Faith of Abraham** | Hebrews 11:8-16 |
| Tue, Oct. 1 | **The Call of Abram** | Genesis 12:1-7 |
| Wed, Oct. 2 | **Settling in the Land** | Genesis 13:8-18 |
| Thu, Oct. 3 | **The Land and the Covenant** | Genesis 17:1-8 |
| Fri, Oct. 4 | **The Covenant Recounted and Renewed** | Joshua 24:1-13 |
| Sat, Oct. 5 | **The Covenant Remembered** | Psalm 105:1-11 |
| Sun, Oct. 6 | **The Covenant with Abraham** | Genesis 15:5-21 |
| Mon, Oct. 7 | **A Childless Wife** | Genesis 11:27-32 |
| Tue, Oct. 8 | **A Beautiful Wife** | Genesis 12:10-20 |
| Wed, Oct. 9 | **A Threatened Wife** | Genesis 16:1-6 |
| Thu, Oct. 10 | **The Promise of a Covenant** | Genesis 17:18-22 |
| Fri, Oct. 11 | **Dispelling the Competition** | Genesis 21:8-14 |
| Sat, Oct. 12 | **Mourning a Beloved Wife** | Genesis 23:1-6 |
| Sun, Oct. 13 | **Bearing a Child of Promise** | Genesis 17:15-17; 18:9-15; 21:1-7 |



| | | |
|---|---|---|
| Mon, Oct. 14 | **The Promise of Many Descendants** | Genesis 15:1-6 |
| Tue, Oct. 15 | **A Child Born in Affliction** | Genesis 16:7-16 |
| Wed, Oct. 16 | **The Symbol of the Covenant** | Genesis 17:9-14 |
| Thu, Oct. 17 | **Abraham's Test of Faith** | Genesis 22:1-8 |
| Fri, Oct. 18 | **Abraham's Obedience Blessed** | Genesis 22:9-18 |
| Sat, Oct. 19 | **The Blessed of the Lord** | Genesis 26:26-31 |
| Sun, Oct. 20 | **Blessing Two Family Branches** | Genesis 21:12-14, 17-21; 26:2-5, 12, 13 |
| Mon, Oct. 21 | **One Greater than Jacob** | John 4:1-15 |
| Tue, Oct. 22 | **The Plot to Gain a Blessing** | Genesis 27:1-10 |
| Wed, Oct. 23 | **Planning the Deception** | Genesis 27:11-17 |
| Thu, Oct. 24 | **A Blessing Gained Through Deceit** | Genesis 27:18-29 |
| Fri, Oct. 25 | **Jacob Received God's Blessing** | Genesis 32:22-30 |
| Sat, Oct. 26 | **Jacob's Name Changed to Israel** | Genesis 35:9-15 |
| Sun, Oct. 27 | **God's Assurance for Jacob** | Genesis 28:1, 10-22 |
| Mon, Oct. 28 | **Oppression Under a New King** | Exodus 1:7-14 |
| Tue, Oct. 29 | **The King's Evil Plan** | Exodus 1:15-22 |
| Wed, Oct. 30 | **The Sparing of the Infant Moses** | Exodus 2:1-10 |
| Thu, Oct. 31 | **Moses Flees from Pharaoh** | Exodus 2:15-25 |
| Fri, Nov. 1 | **The People Worship God** | Exodus 4:27-31 |
| Sat, Nov. 2 | **Moses' Encounter with God** | Exodus 3:1-6 |
| Sun, Nov. 3 | **Moses' Commission from God** | Exodus 3:7-17 |
| Mon, Nov. 4 | **The Lamb of God** | John 1:29-37 |
| Tue, Nov. 5 | **The Troubles Multiply** | Exodus 5:19-23 |
| Wed, Nov. 6 | **Broken Spirits and Closed Ears** | Exodus 6:2-9 |
| Thu, Nov. 7 | **The Final Plague** | Exodus 11 |
| Fri, Nov. 8 | **The First Passover** | Exodus 12:21-28 |
| Sat, Nov. 9 | **The Lord Delivered Israel** | Exodus 12:43-51 |
| Sun, Nov. 10 | **The Promise to Pass Over** | Exodus 12:1-14 |

# Lesson Cycle Chart

*International Sunday School Lesson Cycle, September 2010–August 2016*

| Year | Fall Quarter (Sep, Oct, Nov) | Winter Quarter (Dec, Jan, Feb) | Spring Quarter (Mar, Apr, May) | Summer Quarter (Jun, Jul, Aug) |
|---|---|---|---|---|
| 2010–2011 | The Inescapable God (Exodus, Psalms) | Assuring Hope (Isaiah, Matthew, Mark) | We Worship God (Matthew, Mark, Philippians, 1 & 2 Timothy, Jude, Revelation) | God Instructs His People (Joshua, Judges, Ruth) |
| 2011–2012 | Tradition and Wisdom (Proverbs, Ecclesiastes, Song of Solomon, Matthew) | God Establishes a Faithful People (Genesis, Exodus, Luke, Galatians) | God's Creative Word (John) | God Calls for Justice (Pentateuch, History, Psalms, Prophets) |
| 2012–2013 | A Living Faith (Psalms, Acts, 1 Corinthians, Hebrews) | Jesus Is Lord (John, Ephesians, Philippians, Colossians) | Undying Hope (Daniel, Luke, Acts, 1 & 2 Thessalonians, 1 & 2 Peter) | God's People Worship (Isaiah, Ezra, Nehemiah) |
| 2013–2014 | First Things (Genesis, Exodus, Psalm 104) | Jesus and the Just Reign of God (Luke, James) | Jesus' Fulfillment of Scripture (Pentateuch, 2 Samuel, Psalms, Prophets, Gospels, Acts, Revelation) | The People of God Set Priorities (Haggai, Zechariah, 1 & 2 Corinthians) |
| 2014–2015 | Sustaining Hope (Job, Isaiah, Jeremiah, Ezekiel, Habakkuk) | Acts of Worship (Psalms, Daniel, Matthew, Luke, John, Ephesians, Hebrews, James) | The Spirit Comes (Mark, John, Acts, 1 Corinthians, 1–3 John) | God's Prophets Demand Justice (Isaiah, Jeremiah, Ezekiel, Amos, Micah, Zechariah, Malachi) |
| 2015–2016 | The Christian Community Comes Alive (Acts) | Sacred Gifts and Holy Gatherings (Pentateuch, Song of Solomon, Hosea, Micah, Gospels) | The Gift of Faith (Mark, Luke) | Toward a New Creation (Zephaniah, Romans) |

| "God" | "Hope" | "Worship" | "Community" | "Tradition" | "Faith" | "Creation" | "Justice" |
|---|---|---|---|---|---|---|---|

# A Passion for Teaching

*Teacher Tips by Brent Amato*

In any teacher training, should we not consider inspiration before implementation, motivation before methodology, passion before presentation? Think about teachers who have captivated you. I suspect one characteristic of those teachers was their sincere enthusiasm that flowed from hearts passionate about their role.

There are three major sources of passion for Christian teaching. These three are available to all who aspire to be excellent teachers.

## Who Is Teaching: You in Christ!

Realize in the truest and best sense that it is not *just you* who is teaching, but rather *you in Christ*. This "you" is filled with the Holy Spirit (1 Corinthians 6:19; Galatians 2:20). Always keep in mind your spiritual resources for teaching. This means moving beyond secular, human-based credentials to spiritual, God-based power (1 Corinthians 2:1, 3-5; Colossians 3:16). This enables you to identify your insecurities and anxieties about teaching so you can give them over to the Lord (1 Peter 5:7). When you do, you can move beyond Moses' self-doubting responses to God's call (Exodus 3:11; 4:10, 13) to confident acceptance of that call.

Realize that your role is more than a teacher—you are nothing less than a steward of the gospel (compare 1 Corinthians 4:1, 2; 1 Timothy 1:11, 12)! Be faithful and teach, looking forward to the day you will hear the commendation of our Lord: "Well done, thou good and faithful servant" (Matthew 25:21, 23).

Realize also that we cannot fully comprehend the impact of a Spirit-filled, spiritually gifted teacher (John 14:12). *Passionately teach!*

## What You Are Teaching: God's Word!

Realize that you are teaching nothing less than the Word of God (1 Thessalonians 2:13)! When you hold your Bible in your hand, think of yourself as Moses holding the tablets at Mount Sinai. The Bible is the inspired Word of God (2 Timothy 3:16a). The Word of God identifies and meets your students' deepest needs (Hebrews 4:12).

Realize that the Bible is profitable for all whom you teach (2 Timothy 3:16b, 17); it will not fail to accomplish God's purpose for them (Isaiah 55:11). *Passionately teach!*

## Whom You Are Teaching: Your Students!

Realize that you are influencing your students individually and corporately in your church. Realize also that your students may change from week to week in the ways they respond and react to the sown Word. Like Peter, one student may walk into class as a coward in the courtyard one week (Matthew 26:69-75), but as a bold preacher in a public forum the next (Acts 2:14-36). Like Thomas, another student may come as a person of great courage one week (John 11:16), as a doubter the next (20:24, 25), and as a devout worshipper the third (20:26-28).

Realize the truth in the observation, "Everyone is a potential winner. Some people are disguised as losers; don't let their appearance fool you." God knows which students will yield that hundredfold crop (Matthew 13:8, 23), so let Him worry about that. Your goal as a teacher should be that every lesson will promote spiritual maturity for the building of the body of Christ as you sow the Word (Ephesians 4:11-16). *Passionately teach!*

## Teaching as a Passion

Realize how awesome it is for a Christian to be privileged to teach the Bible to others! Make it your goal to be like Apollos, who not only was "fervent in the spirit and taught diligently the things of the Lord" (Acts 18:25), but also was open to being taught "the way of God more perfectly" (18:26). The old cliché "leaders are readers" includes the idea that teachers never stop learning. This too is part of your passion to teach.

# God Creates

**Devotional Reading:** Matthew 6:25-34
**Background Scripture:** Psalm 104

## Psalm 104:5-9, 24-30

**5 Who laid the foundations of the earth, that it should not be removed for ever.**

**6 Thou coveredst it with the deep as with a garment: the waters stood above the mountains.**

**7 At thy rebuke they fled; at the voice of thy thunder they hasted away.**

**8 They go up by the mountains; they go down by the valleys unto the place which thou hast founded for them.**

**9 Thou hast set a bound that they may not pass over; that they turn not again to cover the earth.**

. . . . . . . . . . . . . . . . . . . . . . . . .

**24 O Lord, how manifold are thy works! in wisdom hast thou made them all: the earth is full of thy riches.**

**25 So is this great and wide sea, wherein are things creeping innumerable, both small and great beasts.**

**26 There go the ships: there is that leviathan, whom thou hast made to play therein.**

**27 These wait all upon thee; that thou mayest give them their meat in due season.**

**28 That thou givest them they gather: thou openest thine hand, they are filled with good.**

**29 Thou hidest thy face, they are troubled: thou takest away their breath, they die, and return to their dust.**

**30 Thou sendest forth thy spirit, they are created: and thou renewest the face of the earth.**

## Key Verse

*O Lord, how manifold are thy works! in wisdom hast thou made them all: the earth is full of thy riches.*

**—Psalm 104:24**

Photo: Jupiterimages / Photos.com / Thinkstock

# FIRST THINGS

## Unit 1: First Days

LESSONS 1–5

## LESSON AIMS

After participating in this lesson, each student will be able to:

1. List evidence of God's ability to create and sustain.

2. Match elements of the lesson text with their parallels in Genesis 1 and 2.

3. Write a poem or song of praise to God for His provision and sustaining power.

## LESSON OUTLINE

Introduction
- A. First Things First
- B. Lesson Background: The Psalms

I. Sovereign Power (PSALM 104:5-9)
- A. Creating the Earth (v. 5)
- B. Commanding the Waters (vv. 6-9)
  - *Breathtaking!*

II. Sustaining Care (PSALM 104:24-30)
- A. Providing Variety (vv. 24-26)
  - *His Creativity, Our Blessing*
- B. Providing Food (vv. 27, 28)
- C. Providing Life (vv. 29, 30)

Conclusion
- A. The Importance of Beginning Well
- B. Prayer
- C. Thought to Remember

## Introduction

### A. First Things First

Being first at something is generally considered a mark of distinction. To be the first in one's family to graduate from college or to be the first runner to cross the finish line are noteworthy.

Sometimes being first implies being a pacesetter or establishing a pattern that others will follow. When Neil Armstrong became the first human to set foot on the moon, it marked a dramatic step forward in the American space program. Jackie Robinson's becoming the first African-American to play major league baseball in 1947 opened the door for other African-Americans to do the same.

The first book of the Bible, Genesis, begins with the familiar "In the beginning God created the heaven and the earth" (Genesis 1:1). It is with good reason that the first "main character" in the Bible is God. As the Creator, He is the ultimate "first." In this case, it is impossible for anyone to imitate His "firstness" even remotely. Hear His words given through the prophet Isaiah: "Thus saith the Lord the King of Israel, and his redeemer the Lord of hosts; I am the first, and I am the last; and beside me there is no God" (Isaiah 44:6). The only one who has ever made a similar claim truthfully is Jesus, who was God "made flesh" (John 1:1, 14; Revelation 1:17; 22:13).

### B. Lesson Background: The Psalms

Today's lesson deals with God's creative activity as described in Psalm 104. The Psalms have been described as "Israel's hymnal"; as such they cover a wide range of topics, just as any church hymnal does.

One of these topics is creation—and specifically God's glory and splendor as seen throughout His creation. Psalm 19:1-6 is a prime example of this; the first verse affirms, "The heavens declare the glory of God; and the firmament sheweth his handywork." Psalm 104 (today's text) is an especially sweeping tribute to God as Creator. Nearly all of its 35 verses highlight the ways in which He demonstrates His loving care for all He has made.

When discussing authorship of the Psalms, many automatically think of King David. That is certainly appropriate since 73 of the 150 psalms are attributed to David in their titles. Two other psalms that have no title are credited to David in the New Testament: Psalm 2 (in Acts 4:25, 26) and Psalm 95 (in Hebrews 4:7). A psalm without a title is often referred to as an "orphan psalm." That is the case with Psalm 104, today's text. But that fact does not detract from its ability to instruct us about God (see 2 Timothy 3:16).

## I. Sovereign Power

(Psalm 104:5-9)

Psalm 104 begins and ends with the writer exhorting himself to bless the Lord; this is parallel to Psalm 103, which begins and ends the same way. In the first four verses of Psalm 104, we can see in poetic language the theme of this preaching-to-self: God is pictured as "clothed with honour and majesty" (v. 1); light is His "garment" (v. 2). He is portrayed as a master designer and builder "who stretchest out the heavens like a curtain" (v. 2) and lays the "beams of his chambers in the waters" (v. 3; these are the waters "above the firmament" in Genesis 1:7) as though the heavens were a building with various levels or "floors."

He also makes the clouds His "chariot," and He walks "upon the wings of the wind" (Psalm 104:3). Paganism uses chariot imagery in descriptions of certain fictional deities; such imagery is used here (and elsewhere in Scripture) to present the Lord as the supreme one. He in truth holds the power that they hold only in myth. Only He can make "his angels spirits; his ministers a flaming fire" (v. 4; compare Hebrews 1:7).

## HOW TO SAY IT

| | |
|---|---|
| Baal | *Bay*-ul. |
| Canaan | *Kay*-nun. |
| Canaanite | *Kay*-nun-ite. |
| Elijah | Ee-*lye*-juh. |
| Elisha | Ee-*lye*-shuh. |
| Galilee | *Gal*-uh-lee. |
| Haggai | *Hag*-eye or *Hag*-ay-eye. |
| leviathan | luh-*vye*-uh-thun. |
| Noah | *No*-uh. |

### A. Creating the Earth (v. 5)

**5. Who laid the foundations of the earth, that it should not be removed for ever.**

The picture of God as the divine architect continues. The Scriptures teach that at the end of time, when Jesus returns, the old earth will indeed be removed (2 Peter 3:10). What the psalmist is saying is that no human being—no power other than that of the Creator himself—can remove or move the earth from its established position.

The earthquakes that occur throughout the world should caution us against placing too much trust in "things on the earth" (Colossians 3:2). The writer of Hebrews contrasts the shakiness of this world with the kingdom of God, which "cannot be moved" (Hebrews 12:26-28; compare Haggai 2:21). It just stands to reason that the one who *laid the foundations of the earth* has the ability to move or remove it whenever He wishes.

*What Do You Think?*

Does the way you pray match the way you *should* pray when the world seems out of control? Why, or why not?

*Talking Points for Your Discussion*

- During crises that touch you personally
- During crises that don't touch you personally

### B. Commanding the Waters (vv. 6-9)

**6. Thou coveredst it with the deep as with a garment: the waters stood above the mountains.**

Previously in this psalm, God is portrayed as clothing himself with honor and majesty, covering himself with light (vv. 1, 2). Here He covers the earth *with the deep*—that is, with deep waters—that at one time *stood above the mountains.* This appears to describe the setting of Genesis 1:2: "And the earth was without form, and void; and darkness was upon the face of the deep." At that point nothing was visible except the waters.

**7, 8. At thy rebuke they fled; at the voice of thy thunder they hasted away. They go up by the mountains; they go down by the valleys unto the place which thou hast founded for them.**

The waters are characterized almost as a rebellious child; they receive a rebuke from the Lord, and in response they flee to their assigned places. Thunder is often associated with pagan deities in antiquity, but the Scriptures tell us that thunder is the voice of God. Psalm 29:3 in particular notes, "The voice of the Lord is upon the waters: the God of glory thundereth: the Lord is upon many waters" (compare 2 Samuel 22:14; Job 37:4, 5; Psalms 18:13; 77:18). It is interesting to see the idea of God's thunderous voice alongside that of His self-adornment with majesty, etc., in Job 40:9, 10.

We should also consider what the Old Testament says about God's sovereignty over creation in contrast with how the pagan peoples of Old Testament times view the world. For pagans, the world is often a fearsome, terrifying place. Natural disasters are seen as an indication that "the gods" need to be appeased in some way. The peoples who worship these fictitious gods are not sure what they have done to cause the gods' wrath. Consequently, these people live in a state of perpetual uncertainty regarding the gods they worship.

The Old Testament, however, is quite clear in its acknowledgment of the world as the creation of the one true God, who is personal, powerful, and sovereign. He is to be trusted and faithfully served by those made in His image. The ancient Israelites are not a seafaring people, yet they know that the sea is not a place of uncontrolled chaos. Like everything else in the world, the waters are the handiwork of God.

Visual for Lesson 1. *Point to this visual as you ask, "How has your study of creation helped you better appreciate the Creator?"*

*What Do You Think?*

How will you use this passage to remind yourself that God is in control?

*Talking Points for Your Discussion*

- In times of physical uncertainty (natural disasters, health problems, etc.)
- In times of relational uncertainty (divorce, etc.)
- In times of spiritual uncertainty (satanic attack, etc.)
- Other

### *Breathtaking!*

On the Enhanced Fujita Scale, an EF5 tornado is the most destructive. The year 2011 saw several of these devastate various areas of Mississippi, Alabama, Tennessee, Missouri, and Oklahoma. At the heart of the affected areas, it didn't matter how well the homes were built. The EF5 funnels leveled everything.

How small we feel when we view the forces of nature! How much more difficult it is to imagine the power that creates and maintains all that is! How can we quantify the power of the Almighty? How can we grasp its magnitude? It's possible to read the poetry of Psalm 104 and miss the reality of it. The Lord truly can control the forces of nature with a word. In His perfect expression of the Almighty Father, Jesus spoke to a storm and calmed it (Matthew 8:23-27).

Knowing that the master of all elements and forces is watching us should draw us to godly fear and reverence. Knowing that His powerful love and grace work continually to draw us back to Him should take our breath away. —V. E.

**9. Thou hast set a bound that they may not pass over; that they turn not again to cover the earth.**

Again we see an affirmation of God's control over His creation. "This is my Father's world" is what an old hymn declares, and thus it has always been. The waters go to their appointed places; they do not act independently of their Creator. This verse describes what happens in Genesis 1:9: "And God said, Let the waters under the heaven be gathered together unto one place, and let the dry land appear: and it was so."

The language of this verse could also apply to the flood of Noah's day (see lesson 4). The statement that the waters will *turn not again to cover the earth* is reminiscent of God's promise to Noah and his sons following the flood (Genesis 9:11, 15).

In addition, the prominence of water in these verses and the emphasis on God's control of them calls to mind the various miracles in the Bible involving water. Included in this list is the parting of the Red Sea to allow the Israelites to escape the Egyptians (Exodus 14:21, 22; see lesson 12), the parting of the Jordan River to allow the Israelites to enter Canaan (Joshua 3:14-17), the parting of the Jordan by both Elijah and Elisha (2 Kings 2:8, 13, 14), and Jesus' stilling of a storm on the Sea of Galilee (Mark 4:35-39). The "rebuke" in Psalm 104:7 may be compared with Jesus' command of "Peace, be still," which brought immediate calm to that storm.

## II. Sustaining Care

(Psalm 104:24-30)

While the first part of our printed text highlights God's work in creation, the next portion describes God's faithfulness in sustaining His creation. The psalmist calls attention to this in verses 10-23 (not in today's text), where he gives examples of God's providential care on earth and in the heavens. All of this bears witness that what people often call "the natural world" is in reality "the supernatural world," for it all exhibits the gracious hand of God.

### A. Providing Variety (vv. 24-26)

**24. O Lord, how manifold are thy works! in wisdom hast thou made them all: the earth is full of thy riches.**

The psalmist pauses in the midst of his examples of God's care for His creation to reflect on and extol God's many wonderful works. The Creator is indeed creative! This is abundantly clear from the variety of creatures in the world. The distinctions in size, color, speed, and other characteristics are amazing! Humans in their limited wisdom have studied and categorized these creatures; but at the same time, sadly, people often have failed to give credit to the wisdom that made these creatures in the first place.

That wisdom is God's alone. May we never lose our sense of wonder at our Creator's magnificent craftsmanship. Such variety provides a vast source of riches for us to enjoy—the kind of wealth that has nothing to do with the size of one's bank account!

*What Do You Think?*

What situations other than Sunday worship prompt you to praise God? Why?

*Talking Points for Your Discussion*

- With family
- Among friends
- At work
- Alone
- Other

### *His Creativity, Our Blessing*

My husband is an entomologist. Because of this, I have learned more about insects than I ever thought I would. Did you know there are more varieties of beetles—more than 350,000 types—than all of the other types of creatures combined? There are certainly even more that humans have yet to discover.

Bugs aren't the only place to notice variety. Our family has relocated many times, and whenever we meet new neighbors and coworkers, we find that each person is unique. We have never found a duplicate.

Psalm 104 points to the Father's creativity. He delights in variety. He never runs out of fresh ideas and ways to bless us. It is criminal for us to put God in a box of our limited understanding, to think He cannot show us the way out of our current challenges. It will take all of eternity to fathom and enjoy the infinite facets of His wisdom. But it is our privilege to praise Him and His ways *now.* Indeed, we fail in our role as children of God when we neglect to praise Him for the many wonders He has placed in the ample "playground" He has made for us. —V. E.

**25. So is this great and wide sea, wherein are things creeping innumerable, both small and great beasts.**

The psalmist now focuses on one area of creation where variety is especially evident: the *great and wide sea*. Documentaries that have filmed ocean life have captured some of this for all to see. These programs provide us with a sense of just how impressive are the number and size *(both small and great)* of the creatures that dwell in the waters. The psalmist acknowledges this, even without the benefit of the technology we possess today.

> *What Do You Think?*
> How do modern discoveries affect your view of God and His creation?
>
> *Talking Points for Your Discussion*
> - Regarding living organisms
> - Regarding forces of nature
> - Regarding psychology
> - Regarding secular views of evolution
> - Other

**26. There go the ships: there is that leviathan, whom thou hast made to play therein.**

Certain occupations allow people to appreciate in a special way the magnitude and wonder of God's creative activity. Here the psalmist describes those who travel in ships as having a special window through which to see the splendor of creation. In particular *that leviathan* is cited as a creature that God has *made to play* in the waters.

What exactly is a leviathan? Obviously it is some kind of creature of the water, though specifically which one is subject to much speculation. Some think it is a crocodile. Job 41, where leviathan is described in much more detail, may support this. In particular, Job 41:14 notes that "his teeth are terrible round about" (with *terrible* meaning "capable of inciting terror"). However, Job 41 also uses much figurative language in describing leviathan (see vv. 18-21), so we are cautious about making a firm identification. The notation regarding "the heads of leviathan" in Psalm 74:14 adds to our caution.

In any case, leviathan is clearly a creature to be feared according to the way Job 41 pictures it. Isaiah 27:1, a passage where the judgment of God is described, mentions "the piercing serpent, even leviathan that crooked serpent." This seems to connect leviathan with the serpent as the latter is used in Scripture to portray Satan.

Accounts from ancient Canaanite literature mention a many-headed sea serpent that is defeated by the god Baal. Here in Psalms, though, the focus is more on leviathan as simply a creature of the water—just one of many that God has created. And leviathan is clearly under the control of the Creator, who considers it as one of the many creatures He allows *to play* in His "swimming pool."

Perhaps a connection to pagan myths is a part of the psalmist's reason for mentioning leviathan; the psalmist may want to convey that the true God, the Creator, is far superior to any power associated with paganism. Since the true God has created the sea creatures, any discussion of a god needing to defeat a sea serpent is laughable.

### B. Providing Food (vv. 27, 28)

**27. These wait all upon thee; that thou mayest give them their meat in due season.**

All creatures depend on the Lord. How sad that humans, though made in the image of God, often refuse to acknowledge Him as the giver of "every good gift and every perfect gift" (James 1:17). Worse still is our tendency to complain about God's provisions from time to time (compare Numbers 11:6).

> *What Do You Think?*
> What effort will you make in the week ahead to turn your complaints into praise?
>
> *Talking Points for Your Discussion*
> - While stuck in traffic
> - In seeing high prices while grocery shopping
> - While working in an unfulfilling job
> - Other (be specific)

**28. That thou givest them they gather: thou openest thine hand, they are filled with good.**

Sometimes we feed certain animals by allowing them to eat from our hands. God's power to give in this regard is infinitely greater than ours. Moses warned the Israelites not to forget that the

Lord is the source of their blessings and cautioned them not to think that "the might of mine hand hath gotten me this wealth" (Deuteronomy 8:17).

### C. Providing Life (vv. 29, 30)

**29, 30. Thou hidest thy face, they are troubled: thou takest away their breath, they die, and return to their dust. Thou sendest forth thy spirit, they are created: and thou renewest the face of the earth.**

The imagery here should stir self-reflection: do we acknowledge our constant, day-by-day need for God? Do we realize just how terrifying our existence would be without His sustaining presence?

The Lord holds the power of life and death over all His creatures. When these creatures die, they *return to their dust* just as humans do (Genesis 3:19; Ecclesiastes 12:7). God's Spirit then provides life to new creatures so that the earth is repopulated with them. It is noteworthy that the Hebrew word translated as *breath* and *spirit* in these two verses is the same. This is part of the parallelism that characterizes so much of Hebrew poetry, a parallelism that may be less evident in a translation. The fact that the psalmist recognizes that God is the one who *renewest the face of the earth* affirms God to be not only the Creator but also as "Re-creator."

The psalmist concludes Psalm 104 with his own expression of praise to the Lord. He will not allow the creatures of this world to outpraise him! "I will sing unto the Lord as long as I live: I will sing praise to my God while I have my being" (v. 33). The concluding declaration in verse 35 is this: "Let the sinners be consumed out of the earth, and let the wicked be no more." Those who deny God's creative activity or seek to squelch the witness of creation to His greatness will themselves be squelched. The undeniable truth is that God is the Creator. Humanity ignores or defies that fact to its own destruction (compare Daniel 4:28-32).

## Conclusion

### A. The Importance of Beginning Well

In the classic movie *Mary Poppins,* a very proper nanny offers her services to the Banks household, where two rather impudent children live. One of the chores the children need to attend to is cleaning their rooms. To encourage the children to get this task done, Mary presents it as a game—a game she calls, "Well Begun Is Half-Done." Her point is that starting any job properly is the key to completing it well and on time.

The importance of the "well begun" principle can also be applied to the understanding of one's purpose for living. If we have no sense of beginnings or origins or cannot with confidence answer the question, "How did we get here?" then the reason for our existence is shrouded in mystery. So, for that matter, is the issue of our future. If we do not know where we came from, how can we know for sure where we're going? But if we know our beginnings, then we are more than "half done"; we are well on our way to grasping our purpose for living and to knowing what the future holds.

This lesson begins a series of studies entitled "First Things." We should think of *first* not just in terms of things that happened first (in a chronological sense), but also in terms of what is of first importance. If God is in control of "first things" (creation), then "middle things" (the present) have purpose, and "last things" (the future) are in His hands as well.

### B. Prayer

Lord of all creation, we join with the psalmist in voicing our praise to You for Your marvelous handiwork. We know that what You have made continues to declare Your glory in spite of humanity's determined efforts to silence that declaration. Thank You for Your constant and faithful care. In Jesus' name, amen.

### C. Thought to Remember

God is the one who creates and sustains.

## VISUALS FOR THESE LESSONS

# Involvement Learning

*Some of the activities below are also found in the helpful student book,* Adult Bible Class.
*Don't forget to download the free reproducible page from www.standardlesson.com to enhance your lesson!*

## Into the Lesson

*Option:* Place in chairs copies of the "God's Creation" word-search puzzle from the reproducible page, which you can download. Learners can begin working on this as they arrive.

Create eight large cards with the following entries, one each: *light / sky / land and sea / plants / sun and moon / sea creatures and birds / land animals / man.* Have the following headings displayed on the board as learners arrive: Day 1 / Day 2 / Day 3 / Day 4 / Day 5 / Day 6 / Day 7. Affix the cards to the board randomly. Say, "Let's do a little review. As you can see, I have the elements of creation on the cards. Keep your Bibles closed as we match each to its day of creation. Then we'll check our conclusions with Scripture."

After completing the exercise and checking answers against Genesis 1, say, "Do you know that Genesis 1 is not the only place in the Bible that speaks of creation? This morning we'll look at a parallel passage."

## Into the Word

Divide the class into four small groups or study pairs and make these assignments: Group 1—Psalm 104:5-9; Group 2—Psalm 104:24-30; Group 3—Genesis 1:1-13; Group 4—Genesis 1:14-31. Ask each group to read its assigned text, summarize it, and identify the theme of the passage. When the groups are ready, ask them to share findings. *(Possible responses for summaries and themes: Group 1: an introduction to the creation process / God's power in creation. Group 2: creation of the sea and the creatures that inhabit it / awe at what God has created. Group 3: creation days 1 to 3 / God is the Creator of all that exists. Group 4: creation days 4 to 6 / God's pleasure with all that He created.)* Add information from the commentary to the groups' presentations where appropriate.

When you have completed the Scripture analysis, say, "Sometimes critics of the Bible will claim that passages like these are proof that the Bible is flawed because passages that refer to the same event do not record those events in the same way. Let's see how such passages complement, rather than contradict, one another."

Distribute identical handouts with today's text and Genesis 1:1-31. Ask learners to work in their groups or pairs to put the verses from these two passages into a single sequence so that the two accounts flow as one. *Option:* Distribute scissors and tape so learners can physically arrange the texts. *(Possible compilation: Genesis 1:1→Psalm 104:5→Genesis 1:2→Psalm 104:6→Genesis 1:3-7 →Psalm 104:7, 8→Genesis 1:8, 9→Psalm 104:9→ Genesis 1:10-21→Psalm 104:25, 26→Genesis 1:22-25→Psalm 104:27-30→Genesis 1:26-31.)*

Compare and contrast the results. Differing sequences will provide an opportunity for a close examination of the two passages.

## Into Life

Say, "Our lesson reminds us of the greatness of God and the majesty of His creation. Sadly, God's creation becomes tainted by sin. One kind of sin occurs when people dehumanize others, who are made in God's image." Ask for examples of how this has occurred throughout history; jot answers on the board. *(Possible responses: slavery, genocide, abortion, euthanasia, sex trafficking.)* Discuss ways that "the average person" may be guilty of dehumanizing others; jot answers on the board. *(Possible responses: bigotry, prejudice, stereotyping).* Brainstorm ways to counteract the tendency to dehumanize.

*In addition to or instead of the above:* Distribute copies of the "Mighty Works" activity from the reproducible page; allow three minutes for completion. Discuss results and—in the spirit of a lesson on creation—give a token prize for the most creative set of responses.

Conclude by singing the hymn, "This Is My Father's World."

# God's Image: Male and Female

Devotional Reading: Psalm 8
Background Scripture: Genesis 1, 2; 5:1, 2

## Genesis 2:18-25

18 And the Lord God said, It is not good that the man should be alone; I will make him an help meet for him.

19 And out of the ground the Lord God formed every beast of the field, and every fowl of the air; and brought them unto Adam to see what he would call them: and whatsoever Adam called every living creature, that was the name thereof.

20 And Adam gave names to all cattle, and to the fowl of the air, and to every beast of the field; but for Adam there was not found an help meet for him.

21 And the Lord God caused a deep sleep to fall upon Adam, and he slept: and he took one of his ribs, and closed up the flesh instead thereof;

22 And the rib, which the Lord God had taken from man, made he a woman, and brought her unto the man.

23 And Adam said, This is now bone of my bones, and flesh of my flesh: she shall be called Woman, because she was taken out of Man.

24 Therefore shall a man leave his father and his mother, and shall cleave unto his wife: and they shall be one flesh.

25 And they were both naked, the man and his wife, and were not ashamed.

## Key Verse

*The Lord God said, It is not good that the man should be alone; I will make him an help meet for him.*

—Genesis 2:18

Photo: Stockbyte / Thinkstock

# First Things

## Unit 1: First Days

Lessons 1–5

## Lesson Aims

After participating in this lesson, each student will be able to:

1. Summarize the process by which God created woman.

2. Explain what was "not good" about the man's being alone and what that says about the importance of marriage.

3. Write a note of encouragement to a couple newly married or preparing to enter into marriage.

## Lesson Outline

Introduction
- A. An Unforgettable Wedding
- B. Lesson Background

I. Problem (Genesis 2:18-20)
- A. God States the Need (v. 18)
- B. Adam Sees the Need (vv. 19, 20)

II. Provision (Genesis 2:21-23)
- A. Man Sleeps (v. 21)
- B. God Shapes (v. 22)
- C. Man Speaks (v. 23)
  - *Doing Things God's Way*

III. Principles (Genesis 2:24, 25)
- A. One Flesh (v. 24)
  - *One Weak Moment*
- B. No Shame (v. 25)

Conclusion
- A. The State of the Union (of Marriage)
- B. Singled Out?
- C. Prayer
- D. Thought to Remember

## Introduction

### A. An Unforgettable Wedding

Many weddings took place on April 29, 2011. But one in particular was quite out of the ordinary: the marriage of Prince William to Catherine Middleton. Millions witnessed the ceremony on TV and the Internet; an estimated one million people lined the procession route from Buckingham Palace to Westminster Abbey. Depending on where a person lived, a significant adjustment in one's scheduling was required in order to witness the event as it happened. For example, a pub in Cincinnati, Ohio, opened its doors at 5:45 a.m. so patrons could witness the exchange of vows on its TV.

The lesson text for today records another unforgettable "wedding," if we may use that term. It was unforgettable because it was the very first. This memorable occasion was not witnessed by millions of people. No cheering crowds were there; in fact, only three parties (not counting animals) were present: God, the first man, and the first woman. The account, however, has been read by hundreds of millions of people, for it is recorded in God's sacred Word, in Genesis 2:22, 23.

This record still has much to teach us about the meaning and the significance of marriage. It highlights a truth that today's world desperately needs to recognize: the origin of marriage is divine, not human. It is indeed "holy matrimony."

### B. Lesson Background

Today's lesson and the next three are drawn from the book of Genesis. Today's text deals with part of God's actions on the sixth day of creation. According to Genesis 1:24-31, this is the day God created land animals and the first humans. The picture becomes fuller when we see the first man (Adam) being placed "into the garden of Eden to dress it and to keep it" (Genesis 2:15).

Some students maintain that the creation account in Genesis 2 is an entirely different, and even contradictory, account from that found in Genesis 1. But Genesis 2 should be considered supplementary, not contradictory, to Genesis 1. Some suggest that Genesis 2 is like the effect of a zoom lens, focusing especially on the events of the sixth day, primarily those involving the man and the woman created in God's image.

The focus within Genesis 2 on the creation of the man and the woman is most appropriate given the special place that human beings have in God's creative activity. Only humans are said to be created in the image of God (Genesis 1:26, 27), as what might be called the grand finale of God's work. He saves the best for last, as confirmed by the additional details provided in Genesis 2.

## I. Problem

(Genesis 2:18-20)

### A. God States the Need (v. 18)

**18. And the Lord God said, It is not good that the man should be alone; I will make him an help meet for him.**

The phrase "and God saw that it was good" appears at various stages of His creative work (Genesis 1:10, 12, 18, 21, 25). The assessment of the creation as "very good" concludes the entire account (Genesis 1:31). However, we now learn of a situation that *is not good*: the fact that the man should be alone. So God determines that He *will make him an help meet for him.* The word *meet* in this context carries with it the idea of "appropriate." Therefore the help to be provided for the man is someone who will serve as an appropriate companion.

Thus something of the purpose for the creation of woman is already hinted at even before her creation takes place. She will complete the man, helping him become what he would not be capable of becoming were he to remain alone.

*What Do You Think?*

How can the church do a better job of ministering to those who are now "alone" as widows and widowers?

*Talking Points for Your Discussion*

- In church programming
- In church budgeting
- Cooperating with community-based seniors programs
- Other

### B. Adam Sees the Need (vv. 19, 20)

**19. And out of the ground the Lord God formed every beast of the field, and every fowl of the air; and brought them unto Adam to see what he would call them: and whatsoever Adam called every living creature, that was the name thereof.**

The line *out of the ground the Lord God formed every beast of the field* reflects what has already occurred on the sixth day of creation (see Genesis 1:24, 25). While the waters are said to have brought forth the various sea creatures and birds on the fifth day (1:20), all creatures are made from the ground or dust as noted in Psalm 104:29 (see last week's lesson). The man himself also has been formed "of the dust of the ground" by the Lord God (Genesis 2:7).

But now we come to new information: all of the creatures that God has made are brought before Adam for naming by the man. We wonder if this naming procedure includes each and every subcategory of creature "after his kind" (Genesis 1:25). Some think that that would take too long for a single day, so they propose that Adam names only the broader categories of animals and birds rather than the much more numerous subcategories.

It is noteworthy that this verse includes the first time in the Genesis account that the name *Adam* appears. In the Hebrew text, the word *Adam* is actually the same as that which is translated "the man" in Genesis 2:18 (the Hebrew language has no capital letters to designate proper names). Of perhaps greater significance at this time is the fact that the name *Adam* comes from the Hebrew word meaning "ground" in Genesis 2:7. This calls attention to the material from which he is created.

**20. And Adam gave names to all cattle, and to the fowl of the air, and to every beast of the field; but for Adam there was not found an help meet for him.**

Adam proceeds to name the various creatures. But in the process a sobering truth dawns: although they come from the ground as he does, none is quite like him. *For Adam there was not found an help meet for him.* Thus the state of being alone, which God has already said is "not good" for the man, is recognized by the man himself.

Perhaps we have been wondering to this point why God doesn't just name all the creatures himself. This may be the reason: having Adam do the naming allows him to come to his own conclusion regarding his need.

## II. Provision

(Genesis 2:21-23)

### A. Man Sleeps (v. 21)

**21. And the Lord God caused a deep sleep to fall upon Adam, and he slept; and he took one of his ribs, and closed up the flesh instead thereof.**

God now acts to address the man's incompleteness. This is a multistep process, the first of which is for God to cause *a deep sleep to fall upon Adam.*

The Hebrew word rendered *deep sleep* is used in two other places where the Lord acts in a literal, physical way on individuals: regarding Abram in Genesis 15:12 (lesson 6), and regarding Saul and his companions in 1 Samuel 26:12. (Other uses of this word are found in Job 4:13; 33:15; Proverbs 19:15; and Isaiah 29:10.) It is during this divinely induced anesthesia that the Lord proceeds to the next two steps: removing one of Adam's ribs, then closing the flesh.

### B. God Shapes (v. 22)

**22. And the rib, which the Lord God had taken from man, made he a woman, and brought her unto the man.**

This very brief account of God's creation of a woman raises a question: why create the woman from the man's rib? Many have suggested a special symbolism: woman is made from the "side" of the man so that she will be neither "above" him nor "beneath" him, but always by his side to encourage him. The Bible is silent regarding such symbolism. Scripture simply pulls back the curtain on this very sacred moment, gives us a quick glimpse of what happens, and then closes the curtain. We would not know of this account at all had not God chosen to reveal it to us.

The primary point behind the description of the woman's creation seems to be the special care that God takes to solve the man's incompleteness. The woman is not created from the dust of the ground as was the man; rather, she is created from the man. The psychological importance of this fact is revealed in the next verse.

### C. Man Speaks (v. 23)

**23. And Adam said, This is now bone of my bones, and flesh of my flesh: she shall be called Woman, because she was taken out of Man.**

When Adam awakens from his surgery, the recovery time is apparently very brief. He beholds in amazement the new individual before him and immediately understands that she is not like any of the creatures he has previously seen and named. The phrase *This is now* is somewhat difficult to translate from Hebrew into smooth English that will fit with the rest of the sentence. Literally it reads, "This is the time." Perhaps an exclamation such as "At last!" fits the setting.

Adam acknowledges what makes God's newest creation unique: she is *bone of my bones, and flesh of my flesh.* Adam is aware of the procedure he has just undergone. But rather than feel like he is "missing something" (a rib), he experiences a sense of completeness. His feeling of being alone has been remedied. He clearly sees a special individual before him—one with whom he senses a genuine kinship.

Adam then proceeds to "name" this new creation, just as he has previously named the creatures brought before him: *She shall be called Woman.* Earlier we noted that the Hebrew words for *ground* and *Adam* (or *the man*) are drawn from the same noun. Here, however, a different word for *man* is used by Adam when he says of the woman that *she was taken out of Man.* The word for man that is related to the word *ground* will not do here, for this new individual has not come from the ground as Adam has. Since she has been *taken out of Man,* her designation, *Woman,* is taken out of the different word for man that Adam uses (in fact, it is the feminine form of that word).

## HOW TO SAY IT

| | |
|---|---|
| Corinthians | Ko-*rin*-thee-unz (*th* as in *thin*). |
| Ephesians | Ee-*fee*-zhunz. |
| Moses | *Mo*-zes or *Mo*-zez. |

We should note at this point that the name Adam gives his new companion is really more of a description that recognizes what distinguishes her from the other residents in the Garden of Eden. Adam will not actually name her *Eve* until later, after the fall (Genesis 3:20). Out of all the designations that Adam has assigned on this sixth day, we can be sure that *woman* will be the one he will cherish most!

*What Do You Think?*

What are some ways that husbands and wives can use their similarities and differences to become a more complete reflection of the image of God?

*Talking Points for Your Discussion*

- In thoughts (Hebrews 10:24)
- In words (Proverbs 16:24)
- In actions (Galatians 5:13)

### *Doing Things God's Way*

Private citizens and governments around the world are intensely debating the definition of marriage. Can two people of the same gender be married? Isn't it discrimination to view same-sex couples as less than married so long as they are committed to each other? God is love—isn't it unloving to be biased in our view of people?

This question is answered directly in God's Word: God calls homosexual behavior an "abomination" (Leviticus 18:22; compare Romans 1:26, 27; 1 Corinthians 6:9). Today's text reveals the perfect and deliberate design of God: marriage of one man to one woman.

Make no mistake: the cultural trend of redefining marriage involves the twisting of God's design and purpose for marriage and family. God loves every person He has ever made. He always desires what is best for each of us. As His children, we must not behave disrespectfully, but always graciously honor others as His image bearers. But behaviors that God abhors are never to be called "good" (Isaiah 5:20). God does not sanction homosexual relationships; we shouldn't either. The loving thing to do is to point people to God and His ways. —V. E.

## III. Principles

(Genesis 2:24, 25)

### A. One Flesh (v. 24)

**24. Therefore shall a man leave his father and his mother, and shall cleave unto his wife: and they shall be one flesh.**

Moses wrote the first five books of the Bible, and that fact raises a question about this verse: is Moses quoting Adam here, or is this Moses' own inspired commentary? Being the first human, Adam never has the experience of leaving *his father and mother,* thus suggesting that this is Moses' commentary. Of course, the Holy Spirit could inspire Adam to make this statement, but it is probably better to see the words as those of Moses.

Three significant stages in a marriage relationship are set forth in this verse. The first is that *a man [shall] leave his father and his mother.* Marriage involves the creation of a new bond; this is a bond with one's spouse, a bond that supersedes any close ties with parents. This does not mean that no further involvement occurs with the parents; the idea, rather, is that the parental bond is no longer the most significant relationship in the lives of the husband and wife.

Second, the man is to *cleave unto his wife.* The Hebrew word translated as *cleave* means "cling to" or "stick to." It implies an especially tight bonding or loyalty. That is why the first step of fully leaving father and mother must be made. Marriage counselors can attest to the fact that many problems in marriages occur because loyalty to one or both parents continues to trump loyalty to one's spouse.

The third step is a result of the cleaving: the husband and wife become *one flesh.* This speaks primarily to the unity that is to characterize marriage in the sight of God. That oneness is rooted in the process by which woman was created. God actually did make two out of one by creating woman from man's rib; two then become one in marriage. The intimacy that this creates certainly includes the sexual relationship, but it cannot be limited to that. True intimacy means a sharing of every aspect of life lest the oneness be compromised.

*What Do You Think?*

What are some ways for unmarried people to seek fulfillment outside the context of marriage?

*Talking Points for Your Discussion*

- 1 Corinthians 7:7, 8, 32-35
- 1 Timothy 5:9, 10
- Other

The vital importance of Genesis 2:24 is seen in the fact that it is quoted four times in the New Testament (see Matthew 19:1-6 and its parallel in Mark 10:1-8; 1 Corinthians 6:12-20; and Ephesians 5:22-33). These timeless words continue to proclaim God's design concerning marriage: one man and one woman becoming one flesh for life.

*What Do You Think?*

What can couples do to ensure their marriages reflect God's plans and purposes for marriage?

*Talking Points for Your Discussion*

- 1 Corinthians 7:10-16
- Ephesians 5:22-33
- Hebrews 13:4
- 1 Timothy 5:14

### *One Weak Moment*

Shortly after moving our family for a new job, my husband moved us again in order to get a job he would enjoy more. I agreed, but the transition proved to be more difficult than I had expected. While he was enjoying his dream job, I was miserable, struggling to rebuild my life. Then the thought hit me: *I could move back to California—to the place where I enjoyed work, friends, and climate!*

My mother, sister, grandmother, and even great-grandmother had been divorced, so why couldn't I? I was independent, and knew I could survive. There were only two problems with my solution. First, my friends in California were Christians and would not support my leaving my husband for this reason. The second reason was even more troubling: although I knew I could live without a husband, I was sure I couldn't live without God. The Bible is clear that God desires spouses to stay together (Malachi 2:16; Mark 10:9). I just couldn't figure out how to be right with God while choosing not be right with my husband.

When I finally told God "okay," I felt Him lift me out of despair. Looking back, I can't imagine the damage that one decision would have brought me, my children, and my spouse (who happens to be my best friend). My discontentment phase is barely memorable from this point in life. This Scripture shows that marriage is a priority union. This isn't to diminish the value of the extended family, but to show God's point of view for this special, for-life relationship. —V. E.

### B. No Shame (v. 25)

**25. And they were both naked, the man and his wife, and were not ashamed.**

This is an interesting way to conclude this account. The issue of nakedness has not been mentioned thus far, but it will become a critical issue in the next chapter of Genesis, where Adam and Eve's disobedience is recorded. One of the consequences of their sin will be recognizing their nakedness and covering themselves (Genesis 3:7).

At this point, however, innocence characterizes the relationship between the first man and the first woman. The fact that their nakedness produces no sense of shame reflects not only that innocence but also the degree of intimacy between them. When sin intrudes, their innocence will depart. Their intimacy will be damaged badly, as shown by Adam's attempt to blame his wife, in whom he had originally expressed delight (Genesis 3:12, next week's lesson).

*What Do You Think?*

How have you seen sin affect intimacy?

*Talking Points for Your Discussion*

- Between God and people
- Between spouses
- Within the church
- Other

## Conclusion

### A. The State of the Union (of Marriage)

For as long as most of us can remember, God's ideal for marriage has been under assault in Western society. "Living together" (which used to be called "shacking up") has gained acceptance, even from some who have been brought up in the church. No doubt this cavalier attitude toward marriage is just one of many consequences that the Western world has experienced as a result of its rejection of a Judeo-Christian framework that defines marriage on biblical terms.

But this is not the time (nor is it ever) for the church to wave the white flag in surrender. We cannot allow the culture to set the terms of the marriage issue. Churches can offer sermons, retreats, and Bible studies on God's plan for marriage. Premarital counseling can be offered (or made mandatory) to those considering marriage in the church. Youth should be instructed during (or before) the high-school years about the biblical teaching concerning marriage and how the Christian marriage can serve as a model of the relationship between Christ and the church.

That last point is crucial. Ultimately, the assault on marriage undermines a key witnessing tool of the church. Strong marriages are an essential part of how the church witnesses on behalf of Jesus to a lost world (compare 1 Timothy 5:14, 15). When Paul uses marriage to illustrate the relationship between Christ and the church in Ephesians 5, he cites Genesis 2:24. That illustration remains a vital part of the church's message to whatever culture it is confronting. Marriage is meant to honor the Creator, and it is meant to honor the head of the church, Jesus Christ.

### B. Singled Out?

Unmarried Christians who are content to remain single may feel a bit uncomfortable by the declaration, "It is not good that the man should be alone" (Genesis 2:18). They may discover that their lifestyle allows them to serve the Lord with a freedom and flexibility that would not be theirs if they were married.

The single lifestyle is not inconsistent with the overall teaching of Scripture. Paul, whose high regard for marriage we have already noted, told the Corinthians that a married person has additional cares to address (1 Corinthians 7:32-34). Jesus acknowledged that some remain unmarried

Visual for Lesson 2. *Point to this visual as you ask, "What are some things the church can do to uphold and promote the biblical view of marriage?"*

"for the kingdom of heaven's sake" (Matthew 19:12). Genesis 2:18 must be seen in its immediate setting. It was certainly not good for Adam to remain alone for several reasons, among them God's desire for humans to "be fruitful, and multiply, and replenish the earth" (Genesis 1:28). Adam could not do that alone!

Living in a world affected by sin, we know that there are situations where singleness may be the preferred state in which one should live. Jeremiah was told to remain single and childless because of the hard times that God's people were to face (Jeremiah 16:1-4). Marriage would have made that man's prophetic task more difficult. One could even say that God demonstrated mercy toward Jeremiah through His command not to marry or have children: Jeremiah would be spared the heartache of seeing his wife and children suffer, and his family would be spared the heartache of seeing a husband and father suffer.

### C. Prayer

Father, may we give marriage the respect it deserves. In these troubled times, we pray for the strength and courage to speak on behalf of marriage as You created and ordained it. In the name of Jesus, whose bride is the church, amen.

### D. Thought to Remember

Marriage is "holy matrimony"
because it was created by God.

# Involvement Learning

*Some of the activities below are also found in the helpful student book,* Adult Bible Class.
*Don't forget to download the free reproducible page from www.standardlesson.com to enhance your lesson!*

## Into the Lesson

Contact learners in advance to ask that they bring one of their wedding pictures to class. Have participants place their pictures in a basket next to the door as they arrive.

After everyone is seated, mix up the pictures; then show them one at a time, asking learners to identify who is in the picture. Allow those pictured to tell how long they have been married. (If your class is of such a size that many won't be able to see details of the pictures, you can collect pictures in advance and scan them for projection.)

*Alternative:* Place in chairs copies of the "Match the Phrases" exercise from the reproducible page, which you can download. Learners can begin working on this as they arrive. Wrap up either this segment or the one above by saying, "Even though today's Scripture will be very familiar to many of us, we want to make sure we study it in the context of marriage."

## Into the Word

Divide the class into four small groups or study pairs; distribute the following instructions: *Task Group*—Identify a task that God gave the first man to perform in today's text and a negative result of that task. *Not-Good Group*—Identify what God declared to be "not good" at the stage of the creation account in today's text; also identify God's solution. *Marriage Group*—Identify what is to happen when people get married. *Process Group*—Describe the steps of the process by which woman was created and Adam's reaction.

Ask groups to present their findings. *(Expected responses: Task Group—task was to name the creatures; negative result was that no "help meet" for the man was found [Genesis 2:19, 20]. Not-Good Group—the man was alone; God would provide a "help meet for him" [2:18]; Marriage Group—attachment to spouse is to supersede attachment to parents, sometimes called "leave and cleave" [2:24, 25]; Process Group—the steps were deep sleep, rib removal, closure of wound, creation of woman, and Adam's recognition of "flesh of my flesh" [2:21-23].)*

Use the following discussion questions to explore the text more fully. You can use these either for a whole-class discussion or as assignments to small groups.

1. What significance is there in the fact that God allowed Adam to be aware of his need before God filled it? *(Genesis 2:20b)*

2. What significance is there in the fact that the creation procedures for the first man and the first woman were different? *(Genesis 2:7, 21, 22)*

3. Why is the need to sever ties with parents an important foundation for a God-honoring marriage? *(Genesis 2:24a)*

4. What does "one flesh" signify in addition to the sexual aspect of marriage? *(Genesis 2:24b)*

After the discussion, say, "I hope that today's lesson has made us more aware of the importance to God of marriage. Now let's put this knowledge into action."

## Into Life

Work together as a class to make a list of best practices for keeping a marriage strong; expect responses from personal experience, from books on marriage, and from Scripture. Jot responses on the board. *Option:* If your class does not include engaged couples, you can start this segment by saying, "Let's compile some 'Helpful Hints' from our collective wisdom that we can pass along to engaged couples as they contemplate their forthcoming marriages. I will mail our list to the engaged couples in our church."

*Alternative:* Have learners complete the "Encouragement for Marriage" activity on the reproducible page. Furnish copies of the church directory to assist learners in identifying those to receive the notes. Ask learners to mail their completed notes, or you can collect the notes to mail yourself.

# Knowledge of Good and Evil

Devotional Reading: Deuteronomy 30:11-20
Background Scripture: Genesis 3

## Genesis 3:8-17, 21, 23

8 And they heard the voice of the Lord God walking in the garden in the cool of the day: and Adam and his wife hid themselves from the presence of the Lord God amongst the trees of the garden.

9 And the Lord God called unto Adam, and said unto him, Where art thou?

10 And he said, I heard thy voice in the garden, and I was afraid, because I was naked; and I hid myself.

11 And he said, Who told thee that thou wast naked? Hast thou eaten of the tree, whereof I commanded thee that thou shouldest not eat?

12 And the man said, The woman whom thou gavest to be with me, she gave me of the tree, and I did eat.

13 And the Lord God said unto the woman, What is this that thou hast done? And the woman said, The serpent beguiled me, and I did eat.

14 And the Lord God said unto the serpent, Because thou hast done this, thou art cursed above all cattle, and above every beast of the field; upon thy belly shalt thou go, and dust shalt thou eat all the days of thy life:

15 And I will put enmity between thee and the woman, and between thy seed and her seed; it shall bruise thy head, and thou shalt bruise his heel.

16 Unto the woman he said, I will greatly multiply thy sorrow and thy conception; in sorrow thou shalt bring forth children; and thy desire shall be to thy husband, and he shall rule over thee.

17 And unto Adam he said, Because thou hast hearkened unto the voice of thy wife, and hast eaten of the tree, of which I commanded thee, saying, Thou shalt not eat of it: cursed is the ground for thy sake; in sorrow shalt thou eat of it all the days of thy life.

. . . . . . . . . . . . . . . . . . . . . . . . .

21 Unto Adam also and to his wife did the Lord God make coats of skins, and clothed them.

. . . . . . . . . . . . . . . . . . . . . . . . .

23 Therefore the Lord God sent him forth from the garden of Eden, to till the ground from whence he was taken.

## Key Verses

*And the Lord God said, Behold, the man is become as one of us, to know good and evil: and now, lest he put forth his hand, and take also of the tree of life, and eat, and live for ever: therefore the Lord God sent him forth from the garden of Eden, to till the ground from whence he was taken.* —**Genesis 3:22, 23**

# First Things

## Unit 1: First Days

Lessons 1–5

## Lesson Aims

After participating in this lesson, each student will be able to:

1. Describe the consequences of the sin of Adam and Eve as well as God's promise of hope.

2. Match the descriptions of both the consequences of sin and God's promise of hope with specific examples from modern life.

3. Confess and repent of one "hidden sin" in his or her life.

## Lesson Outline

Introduction
- A. Surviving the Fall
- B. Lesson Background

I. Confronting the Problem (Genesis 3:8-13)
- A. Hearing (v. 8a)
- B. Hiding (v. 8b)
- C. God Addresses the Man (vv. 9-12)
- D. God Addresses the Woman (v. 13)
  - *Rationalizing* vs. *Repenting*

II. Pronouncing Consequences (Genesis 3:14-17)
- A. For the Serpent (vv. 14, 15)
- B. For the Woman (v. 16)
- C. For the Man (v. 17)

III. Enacting the Pronouncement (Genesis 3:21, 23)
- A. Caring for the Couple (v. 21)
  - *Clothing from God*
- B. Casting Out the Couple (v. 23)

Conclusion
- A. The Right Kind of Knowledge
- B. Prayer
- C. Thought to Remember

## Introduction

### A. Surviving the Fall

May 30, 2011, was an unusually hot Memorial Day in the Bronx section of New York City. From the fifth floor of an apartment, 14-month-old Xania Angel Samuels tumbled out of an open window to the ground below. She survived the plunge and was rushed to the hospital with head trauma. Xania had been wearing her favorite pink winter coat when she fell, and the heavy coat—which she insisted on wearing on what was the hottest day of the year to that point—probably cushioned the impact and saved her life.

Today's lesson text from Genesis 3 includes the consequences of what is often termed "the fall" of Adam and Eve, caused by their disobedience to God. Clothing did not protect them from those consequences, but clothing was provided as a part of God's care for them after their fall. Today's text will also show how God looked ahead and foretold a special plan to "cover" all of humanity and shield it from the effects of the fall by administering His own "head trauma" to the serpent.

### B. Lesson Background

Last week we studied God's creation of woman as an appropriate helper for man. A situation that God had previously called "not good" was then made good and complete. But the happy ending of chapter 2 is quickly countered by the opening of chapter 3. The first three words are ominous: "Now the serpent . . ."

Nowhere does the record in Genesis associate the serpent with Satan (the devil). But we know from other Scriptures that the serpent is the instrument of Satan to carry out his hideous designs against the man and the woman, to ruin the perfection that God the Creator established in Eden (2 Corinthians 11:3; Revelation 12:9).

The serpent's first words were intended to cast doubt on the authority of God's word: "Yea, hath God said, Ye shall not eat of every tree of the garden?" (Genesis 3:1). In a blatant denial of the Creator's established consequences for disobedience, the serpent brazenly assured the woman, "Ye shall not surely die" (v. 4). Such a lie is in keeping with the devil's tactics (John 8:44). Tragically, the woman fell into the devil's trap as did the man (Genesis 3:6).

Thus far our consideration of "First Days" in this unit of studies has been positive. It now takes a tragic turn in the opposite direction as we see unfolding before us the chaos that the first sin brings upon the human race and, indeed, all creation. Genesis 3:7 tells us that after the man and the woman had eaten from the forbidden tree, "The eyes of them both were opened, and they knew that they were naked." Thus the consequences of sin are apparent even before the Lord confronts the guilty parties. The innocence and lack of shame that had characterized the man and woman's relationship (2:25) were gone, and they covered themselves with garments made of fig leaves (3:7). Then they had to face the one whose command they had disobeyed.

## I. Confronting the Problem

(Genesis 3:8-13)

### A. Hearing (v. 8a)

**8a. And they heard the voice of the Lord God walking in the garden in the cool of the day.**

It may seem odd that God is described as *walking in the garden,* since "God is a spirit" (John 4:24). The language is most likely a way of portraying the closeness that has characterized the relationship between God and the two humans to this point. One may assume that Adam and Eve's "walk" up to now has pleased God, and they have welcomed the opportunity to walk with Him whenever He comes into the garden. That situation is about to change.

### B. Hiding (v. 8b)

**8b. And Adam and his wife hid themselves from the presence of the Lord God amongst the trees of the garden.**

*Adam and his wife* no longer welcome the sound of God's approach. *The trees of the garden* that have been given to them for their pleasure and enjoyment (Genesis 2:16) are now used as a shield to hide behind. The two are trying to avoid having to face the Lord.

*What Do You Think?*

What are some ways that people "hide" today? How can we grow spiritually from such experiences?

*Talking Points for Your Discussion*

- Hiding behaviors
- Hiding feelings
- Hiding motives
- Other

### C. God Addresses the Man (vv. 9-12)

**9. And the Lord God called unto Adam, and said unto him, Where art thou?**

God already knows where Adam is, of course. God asks *Where art thou?* because Adam needs to know that God desires a word with him.

**10. And he said, I heard thy voice in the garden, and I was afraid, because I was naked; and I hid myself.**

Adam's admission of being afraid signals the end of the closeness that has characterized the relationship that he and Eve have enjoyed between themselves and God to this point. The nakedness that had produced no shame previously (Genesis 2:25) is now a source of shame. Adam is not fully naked at this point since both he and Eve have clothed themselves (3:7). But even though Adam has covered his physical nakedness, he senses that he has not covered it enough to be comfortable in the presence of God.

It is tragically, painfully clear at this point that the serpent has lied. Yes, the eyes of the two humans are open as the serpent had promised (Genesis 3:5, 7); but "knowing good and evil" (v. 5) is not the pleasurable experience that the serpent had led them to believe it would be. Adam "knows" he is guilty of the evil of breaking God's commandment; he "knows" he can no longer be close with God. It would have been far better

## HOW TO SAY IT

| | |
|---|---|
| Corinthians | Ko-*rin*-thee-unz (*th* as in *thin*). |
| Ephesians | Ee-*fee*-zhunz. |
| Xania | *Zan*-yuh. |

for him simply to have trusted and obeyed God than to possess the bitter knowledge that he has acquired through disobedience.

*What Do You Think?*

How do we distinguish between "knowledge of" that honors God and "knowledge of" that doesn't?

*Talking Points for Your Discussion*

- "Knowledge is power." (Francis Bacon)
- "Knowledge is the wing wherewith we fly to heaven." (William Shakespeare)
- "Knowledge is knowing that we cannot know." (Ralph Waldo Emerson)
- "Knowledge puffeth up." (1 Corinthians 8:1)

**11. And he said, Who told thee that thou wast naked? Hast thou eaten of the tree, whereof I commanded thee that thou shouldest not eat?**

Again, it is not information that God seeks as He questions Adam. Rather, the questions are designed to get Adam to realize something. The second of the Lord's questions goes straight to the heart of the matter: has Adam disobeyed the clear command given him by his Creator?

**12. And the man said, The woman whom thou gavest to be with me, she gave me of the tree, and I did eat.**

Adam avoids giving direct answers to the Lord's questions. Instead, Adam points an accusing finger at the woman—the very person whom he had earlier described ecstatically as "bone of my bones, and flesh of my flesh" (Genesis 2:23)! Now it appears that he wants nothing to do with her. Adam even suggests that some blame be placed upon the Lord since Eve is *the woman whom thou gavest to be with me.* Perhaps Adam is implying that being "alone" would not have been such a bad thing after all, in contrast with what the Lord had stated (2:18).

Adam is correct when he says *she gave me of the tree, and I did eat.* That is indeed what happened according to Genesis 3:6. But for Adam to create a scenario that absolves him of all guilt and responsibility is a consequence of the fall that humans continue to practice and perfect. We call it "blame-shifting."

*What Do You Think?*

Under what circumstances are people most likely to shift the blame? How do you resist doing so when the fault is yours?

*Talking Points for Your Discussion*

- Concerning authority figures
- Concerning someone who looks up to us
- Concerning someone we want to impress
- Other

### D. God Addresses the Woman (v. 13)

**13. And the Lord God said unto the woman, What is this that thou hast done? And the woman said, The serpent beguiled me, and I did eat.**

Now God speaks to the woman. The tone appears a bit softer than that used with the man. Perhaps this is because the man had received from the Lord himself the command not to eat from the forbidden tree (Genesis 2:17), while the woman apparently knows of the command from the man. Even so, the woman knew about this command before breaking it (3:2, 3).

Eve admits more of the truth than Adam does. Her statement *the serpent beguiled me* may reveal some blame-shifting on her part, but the key word *beguiled* indicates that she knows that a deception has occurred. The serpent is the source of the deception. The bliss and delight that he implied would belong to the man and the woman are nowhere to be found.

### *Rationalizing vs. Repenting*

One day I heard myself praying (actually, mentally jabbering) about reasons for my behavior. I was doing quite the spin job, if I do say so myself!

Suddenly, it was as if I were listening from another point of view—outside of myself. I could clearly see I had made a mistake and was trying to make myself sound free from guilt. Then a realization struck: God already knew. He knew not only what I had done, but also every subtle nuance of motive behind my behavior. He knew the whole story better than I did myself.

Reclining in my comfortable hearth chair, I paused. It was obvious that my many unspoken thoughts were ridiculous attempts to buoy myself above the rising sense of guilt and shame. Like the prodigal son of Luke 15:11-20, I came to my senses. I asked God to show me His point of view, and the truth of God's Word flooded my mind. I knew where I was wrong and why. Gone was the unease I had felt only minutes before. God's grace was tangible from the first moment I relinquished my excuses and repented (compare Psalm 51).

It's easy to be angry with Adam and Eve. They sinned, and their choice has wreaked havoc on themselves and us. But God is waiting with grace and forgiveness. —V. E.

## II. Pronouncing Consequences

(Genesis 3:14-17)

### A. For the Serpent (vv. 14, 15)

**14. And the Lord God said unto the serpent, Because thou hast done this, thou art cursed above all cattle, and above every beast of the field; upon thy belly shalt thou go, and dust shalt thou eat all the days of thy life.**

Since the serpent has been the instrument of deception, God addresses him first in judgment. God's pronouncement of a curse on the serpent *above all cattle, and above every beast of the field* seems to say that all other creatures will suffer negative effects as a result of sin's entrance into the world (see Romans 8:22, 23), but the serpent will be punished more severely than they.

Some suggest that the words *upon thy belly shalt thou go* imply that the serpent stands upright prior to this curse. But this phrase may mean that the serpent's crawling will now carry with it a meaning of contempt that was not present previously. The idea of eating dust likely signifies humiliation or shame, which it does elsewhere in Scripture (see Psalm 72:9; Isaiah 49:23; Micah 7:17).

**15. And I will put enmity between thee and the woman, and between thy seed and her seed; it shall bruise thy head, and thou shalt bruise his heel.**

The enmity, or hostility, mentioned here is reflected to some extent in the aversion most people have to snakes. But the language of this verse, especially toward the end, points to a deeper spiritual hostility that understands the seed of the serpent to be linked with Satan and all who carry out his evil intentions (compare John 8:44). Satan's continuing desire is to ruin lives by deceit (just as he ruined Eve's), thereby thwarting God's righteous purposes toward those created in His image (compare Revelation 12:9).

In time, however, one seed (descendant) of the woman fulfills God's purpose by dealing Satan a death blow. This is pictured here as striking the enemy's head. Jesus does this by means of His death on the cross (Hebrews 2:14, 15; compare 1 John 3:8). That Satan is to *bruise his heel* indicates that Satan inflicts a measure of suffering on the Son of God, but this in no way causes the kind of damage that Jesus inflicts on Satan.

*What Do You Think?*

How should the fact that Christ crushes Satan affect how we approach our spiritual battles?

*Talking Points for Your Discussion*

- Regarding God's task (Zechariah 4:6; 1 Corinthians 10:13)
- Regarding our task (Ephesians 4:26, 27; 1 Peter 5:8, 9; James 4:7)

### B. For the Woman (v. 16)

**16. Unto the woman he said, I will greatly multiply thy sorrow and thy conception; in sorrow thou shalt bring forth children; and thy desire shall be to thy husband, and he shall rule over thee.**

God turns His attention to the woman. Childbearing was to occur as a part of God's plan prior to the fall (Genesis 1:28), but now the process of multiplying through childbearing will be accompanied by a multiplying of sorrow, referring primarily to the pain involved in giving birth.

Some suggest that a part of this sorrow includes the understanding that any child will enter a world greatly tainted by sin. Who can foresee what aspects of the curse of sin lie ahead for a newborn baby as he or she matures? Despite a parent's best intentions, a child will experience the sorrows of life in a fallen world—and for some that sorrow will be especially tragic.

Another consequence for the woman is stated, one that affects the relationship between husband and wife: *and thy desire shall be to thy husband, and he shall rule over thee.* This has been interpreted in various ways. One idea is that it means she will still desire her husband in spite of the pain of childbirth, and that he will use that to dominate her in the relationship.

It seems better, however, to view this statement as a description of the tension, in the sense of a power struggle, that will characterize the relationship between a husband and a wife as a result of the fall. The harmony and unity that was so eloquently expressed by Adam when the Lord brought the woman to him (Genesis 2:23) will now be a struggle to maintain.

No man should interpret the language of this verse as a license to mistreat his wife. He must honor God in the way he treats his spouse, a principle discussed by Paul, who uses Christ's love for the church as a model (Ephesians 5:25).

### C. For the Man (v. 17)

**17. And unto Adam he said, Because thou hast hearkened unto the voice of thy wife, and hast eaten of the tree, of which I commanded thee, saying, Thou shalt not eat of it: cursed is the ground for thy sake; in sorrow shalt thou eat of it all the days of thy life.**

Now addressing the man, God makes Adam's blame clear: he *hast hearkened unto the voice of [his] wife* rather than to God's voice. Then the man's punishment is pronounced: *cursed is the ground for thy sake.* Like the woman, the man will experience his own version of sorrow; it will come in his efforts to bring forth food from the ground. God had placed the man in the Garden of Eden "to dress it and to keep it" (Genesis 2:15). This task was intended to be a source of satisfaction as the man worked in harmony with his Creator. Now, however, such work will be much more of a drudgery or toil.

Thus the important tasks given for the man and the woman will still be done: children will to be born and crops will be harvested. But the struggle to carry out these duties will always be a reminder of the high price of disobeying God.

## III. Enacting the Pronouncement

(Genesis 3:21, 23)

### A. Caring for the Couple (v. 21)

**21. Unto Adam also and to his wife did the Lord God make coats of skins, and clothed them.**

Following the devastating announcements of discipline, God proceeds to demonstrate an act of grace: He makes *coats of skins* for the couple. The two have already made coverings of fig leaves for themselves (Genesis 3:7), and we wonder if the additional covering of skins foreshadows the system of animal sacrifices that God will institute later. Nothing is said in the Bible about this. The immediate message to Adam and Eve is what should not be overlooked: the God who has just disciplined them still cares deeply for them.

*What Do You Think?*

When was a time that God provided for you in the midst of a problem of your own making? How did Hebrews 12:5-11 apply to that situation?

*Talking Points for Your Discussion*

- Alienating a family member
- Incurring too much debt
- Behaving dishonestly
- Other

### *Clothing from God*

Corporal punishment, time-outs, loss of privileges. Discipline of children can be a controversial topic. Experts seem to agree that the one thing children need when receiving discipline is reassurance of the parent's love. I've seen it dozens of times with children barely old enough to walk: when reprimanded, they rush to the parent's arms. They do so to be reassured that they have not lost the loving relationship with their parent.

The first sin shattered the blissful harmony between God and humans. The consequences pronounced on the first man and woman were surely difficult. What kept the consequences from being unbearable for those two was what God did next. God reassured them of His continuing love by providing them appropriate covering.

God is still busy loving His rebellious children. He sees us attempting to clothe our sin through our own efforts, attempts that end up being only "filthy rags" (Isaiah 64:6). In response, He sends Jesus, who covers our sin with "the robe of righteousness" (61:10). There is probably no better statement of God's love than John 3:16. —V. E.

### B. Casting Out the Couple (v. 23)

**23. Therefore the LORD God sent him forth from the garden of Eden, to till the ground from whence he was taken.**

Perhaps this verse offers one reason why the Lord has clothed the couple: to prepare them for life away *from the garden of Eden*, from which they are now expelled. In verse 22 (not in today's text), God gives the reason for their eviction—so that they, in their fallen condition, will not eat of the tree of life and live forever. This is an act of discipline, but it is also one of grace. Sin-cursed humanity must be protected from itself. Unchecked sin would be catastrophic.

The Hebrew word translated *till* is the same as that translated "dress" in Genesis 2:15. The man will continue to do the work he was doing in the garden, only now he will do so with the grim awareness that the ground from which he has been made is cursed (3:17). He has no one to blame for this sad outcome but himself.

## Conclusion

### A. The Right Kind of Knowledge

Even before Adam and Eve ate of "the tree of the knowledge of good and evil" (Genesis 2:17), there was a sense in which they knew the distinction between good and evil. They knew that eating from the forbidden tree was evil, or wrong. But the serpent implied that something was lacking in their knowledge, and that the Lord was holding out on them. The serpent promised that eating of the tree would open their eyes so they would be "knowing good and evil" (3:5).

After the two had eaten from the tree, the serpent's words partly came true: "And the eyes of them both were opened" (Genesis 3:7). But what did they then "know"? That they were naked.

Visual for Lesson 3

*Use this visual to start a discussion that compares immediate vs. delayed consequences of sin.*

What was their response? "And they sewed fig leaves together, and made themselves aprons."

Consider the irony: the man and the woman, who were then "wise" (moderns might call them "sophisticated") in the realization of their nakedness, proceeded to exercise utter foolishness by trying to cover it up on their own! So whatever "knowledge" they gained was obtained at the price of their ability to think in a spiritually pleasing, God-honoring fashion. Theirs was not the heavenly outcome that the serpent promised; it was hellish, with the loss far, far outweighing whatever gain was achieved.

So it is with any attempt to obtain knowledge apart from our Creator's desires. The irony of Adam and Eve's disobedience and "cover-up" is exemplified by modern humanity's sad plight: we have access to more knowledge than any previous generation, yet spiritually and morally many are woefully ignorant.

### B. Prayer

Father, we live in a time when many freely and proudly boast that they have rejected You. May we who claim to be Your people live lives that will not give them further reason to boast. May our faith in and devotion to You be unmistakably clear. In Jesus' name, amen.

### C. Thought to Remember

Knowledge without God is ultimately ignorance.

# Involvement Learning

*Some of the activities below are also found in the helpful student book,* Adult Bible Class.
*Don't forget to download the free reproducible page from www.standardlesson.com to enhance your lesson!*

## Into the Lesson

*Option:* Place in chairs copies of the "Mixed-up Consequences" activity from the reproducible page, which you can download. Learners can begin working on this as they arrive.

Before class, read a plot overview of the epic poem *Paradise Lost,* by John Milton (easy to find on the Internet). Then print out these three sections of the poem: verses 412–433, verses 734–759, and verses 996–1003 of Book 9. Say, "Today we are going to study the section of Genesis where sin enters the world and humanity is sentenced to suffer its consequences. To set the context, let me read some verses from John Milton's *Paradise Lost.*" (If your learners are not familiar with this classic work, summarize the plot overview for them.) After you have read the three sections from *Paradise Lost,* allow a few minutes for reactions.

*Alternative:* Ask learners to call out the names of public figures whose secret sin was discovered; jot responses on the board. (Save this list for the end of class; put learner responses off to one side because you will need much of the board for the Into the Word segment.) After several names are listed, discuss the consequences each person faced, as well as the ripple effects or collateral damage of his or her sin.

After either opening, say, "Now let's spend some time today studying what the Bible has to say about the immediate and far-reaching consequences of Adam and Eve's choices."

## Into the Word

Mark off the top half of the board in two sections. At the top of the left section, write *Consequences of Sin*; at the top of the right section, write *God's Promise of Hope.* Say, "As we read today's text, be alert to the consequences of Adam and Eve's sin," then ask one or more volunteers to read the text aloud. After the reading, ask learners what consequences of sin they see; jot responses on the board under the left heading. (See the lesson commentary for expected responses.)

After all responses have been entered under the left heading, probe deeper by asking your learners to distinguish between immediate consequences and far-reaching consequences. As learners offer their suggestions, put an *I* next to the entries on the board that are immediate and an *F* next to the ones that are far-reaching. (Immediate consequences are found in verses 8-12; far-reaching consequences are found in verses 14-19, 23.)

Say, "Now let's consider the hope we have, the way out that God provides us from the quagmire of sin." Ask for reactions to verse 15; jot those reactions on the board. Use the lesson commentary on this verse to add information that learners miss.

## Into Life

*Option 1:* If you began the lesson reading from *Paradise Lost,* conclude by reading verses 1–16 and 47b–62 from Book 10 and verses 270–284 and 402–410 from Book 12. Discuss how the poem deals with Christ as the one whom God provides to judge and save Adam and Eve.

*Option 2:* If you began the lesson by asking for a listing of names of public figures whose secret sin was discovered, return to that list now. As a class, discuss what would have been appropriate actions for those individuals to take if they had wanted to repent of their secret sin and guard against its recurrence. (Some of these individuals may have already done so; if that knowledge is available, discuss what they did.) Discuss why repentance and accountability are necessary steps for Christians to take when battling sin.

*Option 3:* Distribute copies of the "No More Secret Sins" activity from the reproducible page. Since this calls for personal confession, you may wish to distribute it as a take-home exercise.

Conclude class with a prayer of thanksgiving for God's provision of salvation through Jesus.

# An Everlasting Covenant

Devotional Reading: Isaiah 54:9-14
Background Scripture: Genesis 6:9–9:28

## Genesis 9:1, 3-6, 8-17

**1 And God blessed Noah and his sons, and said unto them, Be fruitful, and multiply, and replenish the earth.**

. . . . . . . . . . . . . . . . . . . . . . . . . . . .

**3 Every moving thing that liveth shall be meat for you; even as the green herb have I given you all things.**

**4 But flesh with the life thereof, which is the blood thereof, shall ye not eat.**

**5 And surely your blood of your lives will I require; at the hand of every beast will I require it, and at the hand of man; at the hand of every man's brother will I require the life of man.**

**6 Whoso sheddeth man's blood, by man shall his blood be shed: for in the image of God made he man.**

. . . . . . . . . . . . . . . . . . . . . . . . . . . .

**8 And God spake unto Noah, and to his sons with him, saying,**

**9 And I, behold, I establish my covenant with you, and with your seed after you;**

**10 And with every living creature that is with you, of the fowl, of the cattle, and of every beast of the earth with you; from all that go out of the ark, to every beast of the earth.**

**11 And I will establish my covenant with you; neither shall all flesh be cut off any more by the waters of a flood; neither shall there any more be a flood to destroy the earth.**

**12 And God said, This is the token of the covenant which I make between me and you and every living creature that is with you, for perpetual generations:**

**13 I do set my bow in the cloud, and it shall be for a token of a covenant between me and the earth.**

**14 And it shall come to pass, when I bring a cloud over the earth, that the bow shall be seen in the cloud:**

**15 And I will remember my covenant, which is between me and you and every living creature of all flesh; and the waters shall no more become a flood to destroy all flesh.**

**16 And the bow shall be in the cloud; and I will look upon it, that I may remember the everlasting covenant between God and every living creature of all flesh that is upon the earth.**

**17 And God said unto Noah, This is the token of the covenant, which I have established between me and all flesh that is upon the earth.**

## Key Verse

*I will establish my covenant with you; neither shall all flesh be cut off any more by the waters of a flood; neither shall there any more be a flood to destroy the earth.* **—Genesis 9:11**

# FIRST THINGS

## Unit 1: First Days

LESSONS 1–5

## LESSON AIMS

After participating in this lesson, each student will be able to:

1. Summarize what God said about the sacredness of human life in His covenant with Noah and his descendants.

2. Evaluate modern arguments about the death penalty in light of Genesis 9:6.

3. Explain the significance of the rainbow to an unbeliever.

## LESSON OUTLINE

Introduction
- A. Judgment Day
- B. Lesson Background

I. Commands (GENESIS 9:1, 3-6)
- A. Duty (v. 1)
- B. Diet (vv. 3, 4)
- C. Demand (vv. 5, 6)

II. Covenant (GENESIS 9:8-11)
- A. Participants (vv. 8-10)
  - *God's Care*
- B. Promise (v. 11)

III. Confirmation (GENESIS 9:12-17)
- A. Sign (vv. 12, 13)
  - *What Comes to Mind*
- B. Significance (vv. 14-17)

Conclusion
- A. Today's Floods
- B. Prayer
- C. Thought to Remember

## Introduction

### A. Judgment Day

Judgment Day was supposed to occur on May 21, 2011, according to radio preacher Harold Camping. Many of Camping's followers purchased space on billboards throughout the U.S., encouraging people to "save the date" and prepare for the end.

Of course, the date came and went with no judgment except the predictable one that Camping was foolish for having made such a prediction. He was scorned by non-Christians and Christians alike, the latter citing Jesus' clear teaching that no one except God the Father knows the day or the hour of Jesus' return (Mark 13:32). Camping's adjusted prediction for Judgment Day to occur on October 21, 2011, only added to the scorn. Camping turned out to be just another in a long line of "date setters" whose failures proved they were not speaking for God.

Noah, by contrast, received a direct communication from the Lord about a day of judgment—a judgment that was to be carried out by means of a flood. Noah was also told how to prepare for that day, eventually being given an exact timetable as to when God's judgment would be carried out (Genesis 7:4). What made Noah worthy of this honor was the fact that he "was a just man and perfect in his generations, and . . . walked with God" (6:9). Noah obeyed God's commands fully (6:22; 7:5).

While we do not know the time of the coming, final Judgment Day (and we should be extremely suspicious of anyone who claims to know), we *do* know what God's expectations of us are. They are essentially what He has required from His people since day one and what He required from Noah: *obedience.*

### B. Lesson Background

Last week's lesson text focused on the aftermath of the first sin, committed by Adam and Eve in the Garden of Eden. Today's Scripture brings us to the aftermath of God's judgment by means of the great flood. God brought the flood on the world because of the level of corruption and depravity that those made in His image had reached (Genesis 6:5). The exception to this spiritual quagmire was Noah, who "found grace in the eyes of the Lord" (v. 8). God commanded Noah to build an ark, which provided deliverance from the flood for him, his sons, their wives (1 Peter 3:20), and those creatures that Noah was told to take aboard.

The subsequent rains lasted 40 days and nights (Genesis 7:12). Over a year passed from the time the rains began until the earth dried out after the waters receded (comparing 7:11 with 8:13, 14). The Lord then brought forth from the ark Noah, his family, and the living creatures that had been given refuge there. Noah built an altar to the Lord and offered sacrifices (8:20). The Lord responded with a promise that He would never again destroy all living creatures as He had done by means of the flood (vv. 21, 22). The Lord's next words, part of today's printed text, were directed specifically to Noah and his sons.

## I. Commands

(Genesis 9:1, 3-6)

### A. Duty (v. 1)

**1. And God blessed Noah and his sons, and said unto them, Be fruitful, and multiply, and replenish the earth.**

God had made the man and the woman on the sixth day of creation, instructing them to "be fruitful, and multiply, and replenish the earth" (Genesis 1:28). Now, after the judgment carried out through the great flood, God begins what we might call a "re-creation" with *Noah and his sons.* Eight people are to fulfill the mandate given to Adam and Eve (Genesis 7:13; 1 Peter 3:20).

*What Do You Think?*

Do we still have an obligation to "be fruitful, and multiply"? Why, or why not?

*Talking Points for Your Discussion*

- Current world population of seven billion people
- The moral issues of birth control
- Jeremiah 16:1, 2; 29:6
- Luke 23:29
- 1 Timothy 5:14

### B. Diet (vv. 3, 4)

**3. Every moving thing that liveth shall be meat for you; even as the green herb have I given you all things.**

Humanity's diet now is expanded beyond the vegetation permitted in Genesis 1:30, and meat becomes a new source of protein. We may wonder why God gives such permission at this particular time since creatures are not especially numerous. Unclean animals had been taken aboard the ark in twos, while clean animals had been taken by sevens (Genesis 7:2, 3)—and some of the latter have already been sacrificed (8:20). But capture of creatures for food will not be easy since they now fear humans (9:2). It seems that just as man has to "sweat" to produce food from the ground (3:19), he now will be required to exercise a similar effort to obtain meat from earth's creatures.

**4. But flesh with the life thereof, which is the blood thereof, shall ye not eat.**

God next imposes a limitation on the new allowance concerning humanity's diet: people are forbidden to eat *flesh* (or meat) with its blood. The restriction and the reason for it will be restated in the Mosaic law at Leviticus 17:10-14 and Deuteronomy 12:16, 23-25. Taken together, the passages from Genesis, Leviticus, and Deuteronomy imply that blood either is or somehow represents a creature's "life force."

One may suggest that the center of life is in the heart or the brain, but these organs function only if the supply of blood to them is maintained. To cut off the blood supply means certain death. John H. Walton and Victor H. Matthews observe that "the draining of the blood before eating the meat was a way of returning the life force of the animal to the God who gave it life. This offers recognition that [individuals] have taken the life with permission and are partaking of God's bounty as his guests."

Some suggest that this principle remains intact today (compare Acts 15:20, 29). Others point to Jesus' "purging" of all meats (Mark 7:18, 19) as a basis for saying that dietary regulations from the Old Testament are no longer binding. This may be one of those areas where differences of opinion can exist without passing judgment on those who hold them (Romans 14:1-4).

Visual for Lesson 4. *Use this visual to introduce the discussion question that is associated with Genesis 9:16.*

### C. Demand (vv. 5, 6)

**5. And surely your blood of your lives will I require; at the hand of every beast will I require it, and at the hand of man; at the hand of every man's brother will I require the life of man.**

God expands on the previous stipulation. So important is the principle that "life is in the blood" that He states *and surely your blood of your lives will I require.* God will, first of all, require a reckoning for human life that is taken by *every beast* that is responsible for so doing. God declares that He will keep a record of every person killed by a member of the animal kingdom, and He will hold the deadly animal accountable.

Of course, animals do not understand the concept of guilt; even so, they are accountable to their Creator for their actions. How much more, then, is this the case with those created in God's image —beings who *are* capable of understanding guilt! Both this verse and the next address our accountability to God in this regard.

**6. Whoso sheddeth man's blood, by man shall his blood be shed: for in the image of God made he man.**

God requires of humans that the life of a murderer *(whoso sheddeth man's blood)* must be taken as punishment for the heinous act. This principle is later embedded within the Law of Moses, where a distinction is made between premeditated murder and what we would call involuntary manslaughter (Exodus 21:12-14). The reason for the kind of punishment we see in our text is based on our uniqueness as creatures made *in the image of God.* So passionate is God about preserving and protecting this uniqueness that destroying a life must be disciplined to the ultimate degree: life for life (see also Leviticus 24:17; Numbers 35:31).

The Old Testament basis for capital punishment is thus quite clear. To take the life of a murderer is to be considered an act of the utmost respect for life—life as a creative gift of God. Capital punishment is not a barbaric, inhuman act; instead, it is a just response to a deed that has demonstrated the ultimate contempt for the one who creates life.

Capital punishment is controversial today, even within Christianity. Some may question whether the principle of "life for life" is still valid, given the fact that we are no longer under the old law, but are under grace (Romans 6:14). To this concern we can point out that although Jesus has indeed "abolished in his flesh . . . the law of commandments contained in ordinances" (Ephesians 2:15) by "nailing it to his cross" (Colossians 2:14), the requirement of Genesis 9:6 predates the Law of Moses. Further, the New Testament itself seems to indicate that capital punishment is still valid (Romans 13:4; Acts 25:11).

*What Do You Think?*

How does the fact of being made in God's image influence your stand on moral issues today?

*Talking Points for Your Discussion*

- Regarding capital punishment
- Regarding abortion
- Regarding your view of people of other races
- Regarding your response to the needs of those with mental or physical disabilities

## II. Covenant

(Genesis 9:8-11)

### A. Participants (vv. 8-10)

**8, 9. And God spake unto Noah, and to his sons with him, saying, And I, behold, I establish my covenant with you, and with your seed after you.**

God has already told Noah "with thee will I establish my covenant" (Genesis 6:18), the first time the word *covenant* appears in the Bible. Following the great flood, God addresses not only Noah but also his three sons (see 5:32; 6:10; 7:13; and 9:18). God's covenant includes not only them but their *seed,* or descendants (compare 1 Chronicles 1:4-27). Therefore the covenant about to be explained embraces all human beings.

**10. And with every living creature that is with you, of the fowl, of the cattle, and of every beast of the earth with you; from all that go out of the ark, to every beast of the earth.**

God's covenant also applies to *every living creature.* Therefore the prohibitions and warnings that were given earlier regarding these creatures and humans are balanced with the establishment of a special covenant with both parties. The nature of that covenant is explained next.

### *God's Care*

James Herriot was the pen name of James Alfred Wight (1916–1995), an English veterinarian who wrote delightful books about animals and their owners in rural Yorkshire. The books became best-sellers because of their charm and Herriot's winsome manner of describing people and animals.

Herriot's first significant book was *All Creatures Great and Small,* and this title also has been used as the name for a series of four books. He took this title from the nineteenth-century hymn "All Things Bright and Beautiful," of which the refrain's first four lines read as follows:

> All things bright and beautiful,
> All creatures great and small,
> All things wise and wonderful,
> The Lord God made them all.

All four lines became titles of Herriot's books. In these titles, he acknowledges God's creation and His care for all of His creatures.

Genesis records this care. God's promise and covenant to never again flood the entire earth applies also to animals. God's concern for them has a message for us: if God cares for creatures not created in His image, what does this say about His care for those who *are* created in His image? See Matthew 10:29-31. —J. B. N.

### B. Promise (v. 11)

**11. And I will establish my covenant with you, neither shall all flesh be cut off any more by the waters of a flood; neither shall there any more be a flood to destroy the earth.**

The specifics of the Lord's covenant are provided: never again will He use *the waters of a flood* to *cut off* life and *destroy the earth* as He has just done. The next destruction of the earth will be by fire, not water (2 Peter 3:6-12).

*What Do You Think?*

How would you respond to the various ways that people deny *judgment* or *justice* to be an essential aspect of God's nature?

*Talking Points for Your Discussion*

- "God's love means that everyone will be saved in the end."
- "The injustice in the world shows that God doesn't care about justice."
- "Love and judgment are incompatible for God."

## III. Confirmation

(Genesis 9:12-17)

### A. Sign (vv. 12, 13)

**12, 13. And God said, This is the token of the covenant which I make between me and you and every living creature that is with you, for perpetual generations: I do set my bow in the cloud, and it shall be for a token of a covenant between me and the earth.**

Once more the all-inclusive nature of the covenant is emphasized: it is for Noah and his sons (both instances of the pronoun *you* are plural in Hebrew) along with *every living creature.* Moreover, the covenant is *for perpetual generations,* which is another way of describing "your seed after you" in Genesis 9:9 (above).

The visual reminder of the *bow* (or rainbow) is the token of that covenant. The noun *bow* generally describes an instrument of death, used for hunting or warfare (Genesis 27:3; 48:22; etc.). Genesis 9:13, 14, 16 and Ezekiel 1:28 are the only places in the Old Testament where this word signifies a rainbow. Perhaps the symbolism in God's declaration lies in the fact that He is laying aside an instrument of destruction in keeping with His promise not to destroy the earth again by means of a flood.

Some believe that this is the first appearance of a rainbow, marking its significance as part of the covenant that God is establishing. Others maintain that the rainbow has already been seen on previous occasions after rainfalls, but the rainbow becomes the token of God's covenant only after He speaks the words in the verse before us.

*What Do You Think?*

How are modern covenants and contracts different from the covenant in today's text? Why is it important to grasp these distinctions?

*Talking Points for Your Discussion*

- Regarding wedding vows
- Regarding business deals
- Regarding product warranties
- Other

### *What Comes to Mind*

Various cultural myths and symbolisms have been attached to rainbows down through the years. As children we were told that Irish leprechauns place pots of gold at the ends of rainbows; some of us even tried to find such pots. Rainbows are sometimes used in works of art to represent peace and tranquility, with mountain views, buildings, etc., positioned under the rainbow's arc. The unchristian New Age Movement of the latter half of the twentieth century used images of rainbows as part of its identity.

Something is missing in all these representations. It is no mere coincidence that rainbows are formed out of droplets of water suspended in the air—it is, after all, a *rain*bow. God uses rain droplets to remind us that water will never flood the whole earth again.

There is no physical reality to a rainbow since its appearance is due to light passing through water droplets. Yet the lack of physical reality does not detract in the least from God's powerful promise never again to destroy the earth by water. Is that the first thing that comes into your mind when you see a rainbow? —J. B. N.

### B. Significance (vv. 14-17)

**14, 15. And it shall come to pass, when I bring a cloud over the earth, that the bow shall be seen in the cloud: and I will remember my covenant, which is between me and you and every living creature of all flesh; and the waters shall no more become a flood to destroy all flesh.**

God's memory never fails, of course. So the phrase *I will remember* does not imply that God might somehow forget certain details and needs a rainbow to be reminded of them. In a passage such as this, the phrase *I will remember* carries with it the idea that God is about to act to fulfill a promise He has made. A similar usage is found in Exodus 2:24, where God hears the cries of the Israelites in bondage in Egypt and "remembered his covenant." God's response in Exodus 3 is to call Moses to be Israel's deliverer. In the case at hand, God takes personal charge of being the deliverer as He continuously ensures that *the waters shall no more become a flood to destroy all flesh.*

**16. And the bow shall be in the cloud; and I will look upon it, that I may remember the everlasting covenant between God and every living creature of all flesh that is upon the earth.**

This verse reemphasizes what has already been stated. As we ponder what God himself promises to remember, we realize that the rainbow ultimately is meant to help *us* remember something, in the more traditional sense of the word *remember.* God knows how prone we are to forget His works in spite of how great and mighty they are. So He provides memory devices such as the visual aid of a rainbow to help us remember.

*What Do You Think?*

How does each of the following serve to remind you of the promises God has made and how He has kept them?

*Talking Points for Your Discussion*

- The lives of godly people
- The nature of certain places
- The anniversary of a "deliverance event"
- The significance of certain objects
- Other

**17. And God said unto Noah, This is the token of the covenant, which I have established between me and all flesh that is upon the earth.**

A final reaffirmation of the rainbow's importance is given to Noah himself. This is only fitting since this account of the flood began with God's message to Noah about how corrupt the earth had become (Genesis 6:13) and of God's intention to establish His covenant with Noah (6:18).

When Noah is first introduced in Scripture, he is called "a just man and perfect in his generations" (Genesis 6:9). Because Noah faithfully did "according to all that God commanded him" (6:22), he is now given the privilege to witness God's "re-creative" activity and to hear God announce the terms of a covenant with *all flesh that is upon the earth*. It is still true that those who faithfully obey and serve God receive numerous blessings, privileges, and insights that remain only mysteries to those who, like the vast majority in Noah's day, remain entrenched in their wickedness (Matthew 13:10-16; Colossians 1:26).

## Conclusion

### A. Today's Floods

This writer is preparing this lesson during 2011, the rainiest year on record in Cincinnati, where he lives. The months of April and November in 2011 were themselves the wettest Aprils and Novembers on record. This weather pattern caused some parts of the U.S. to suffer greatly from floods and tornadoes. Skeptics may look at a promise of God such as that found in today's text and mockingly ask, "What covenant? Look, I don't care if the flood was worldwide or not; if God is in charge of the world, can't He keep a flood or a tornado from devastating whole towns and communities and disrupting the lives of millions of people? What good can possibly come by His letting such disasters occur?"

Living in a fallen world—a world still under the curse of sin—can present followers of the Lord Jesus Christ with some very challenging questions. We know that ultimately God will bring about "new heavens and a new earth" (2 Peter 3:13). But at times we may wonder why He doesn't step in and fix some of what's wrong with the earth we live in now.

An important part of our witness occurs in the midst of the tragedies that are an inescapable part of life in a fallen world. We are able in such circumstances to show the difference our faith in Christ makes. This is not because we are exempt from tragedies or because life automatically gets better by turning to Jesus. Rather, it is because Christian faith gives us a unique perspective on the tragedies of this present world. The cross of Christ becomes our "token" or sign by which we view life (especially the difficult side) in a fallen world. Just as God used the tragedy of the cross to accomplish His purpose of providing salvation from sin, so He can use the disasters of this life for a higher, eternal purpose (Romans 8:28).

We must remember that we have not had a clear message from God regarding any flood that has occurred since the days of Noah. Noah's flood is the only one specifically tied with the judgment of God. Current floods (and other disasters) can be situations in which Christians demonstrate in tangible ways the love of Christ to cynics. When we do, we allow these circumstances to testify to God's grace rather than His judgment.

### B. Prayer

Father, the covenant You made with Noah is just one example of Your faithfulness. Thank You for the many precious promises found in Your Word. May we find strength and endurance in them whenever life in this sinful world makes us especially weary. In Jesus' name, amen.

### C. Thought to Remember

God is a covenant maker
and a covenant keeper.

## HOW TO SAY IT

| | |
|---|---|
| Colossians | Kuh-*losh*-unz. |
| Deuteronomy | Due-ter-*ahn*-uh-me. |
| Ephesians | Ee-*fee*-zhunz. |
| Leviticus | Leh-*vit*-ih-kus. |
| Mosaic | Mo-*zay*-ik. |
| Noah | *No*-uh. |

# Involvement Learning

*Some of the activities below are also found in the helpful student book,* Adult Bible Class.
*Don't forget to download the free reproducible page from www.standardlesson.com to enhance your lesson!*

### Into the Lesson

Begin class by saying, "Today I thought we'd take a little test to see how well we know the story of Noah's flood. As I read each sentence, raise your hand if the statement is true." (If you think your learners will hesitate to answer publicly in this manner, have them jot their true/false responses on a piece of paper; assure them that you won't collect their answers.)

1. God told Noah to make an ark of oak. *False, Genesis 6:14;* 2. Noah took only two of every animal into the ark. *False, Genesis 7:2, 3;* 3. Noah did exactly as God told him. *True, Genesis 6:22;* 4. It rained for 40 days and nights. *True, Genesis 7:12;* 5. Noah, his family, and the animals left the ark as soon as the rain stopped. *False, Genesis 8:6-10;* 6. Noah sent out a raven to see whether the waters had subsided. *True, Genesis 8:7;* 7. Noah built an altar and offered sacrifices to God after leaving the ark. *True, Genesis 8:20.*

*Alternative:* As a pretest, distribute copies of the "Re-Creation" activity from the reproducible page, which you can download. Allow a few minutes for completing, but don't discuss the results. The correct answers will be apparent as you work through the text in the next segment.

Say, "Even when we've read or heard a text numerous times, there is still much to learn from it. As we study today's text, let's see what new understanding we can gain."

### Into the Word

Before class, reproduce the 15 verses of today's Scripture text on 15 handouts, one verse each. Form learners into pairs or groups of three. Distribute the handouts, as evenly as possible, to the pairs or groups. Ask learners to identify whether there is anything in the verses they have been given that suggests how God views humanity.

Call for conclusions by having a member of each pair or group read a verse aloud and identify the discovery. Jot responses on the board. Responses should resemble the following: *God thinks highly enough of humans to (1) want them to repopulate the earth (v. 1), (2) provide them food (v. 3), (3) want them to view human life as sacred (vv. 4-6), and (4) establish a covenant (vv. 12-17).*

Say, "We can see from Genesis 9:6 that God values human life—so much so that He requires 'life for life' justice. Many today disagree about the appropriateness or validity of the death penalty. Let's consider both secular and Christian arguments for and against capital punishment. What are they?" Write on the board *Secular Arguments* and *Christian Arguments* as two column headings; mark off two areas under each of these as *For* and *Against.* Jot responses in the appropriate areas. Be prepared to challenge learners' positions with observations from the lesson commentary. Remind learners that they must reconcile this issue in light of Scripture, not secular viewpoints.

Wrap up by saying, "Regardless of our personal convictions concerning capital punishment, I think we can all agree that today's text shows us how precious we are to God. How is our value to God connected with the symbol of the rainbow He has granted us to have?" Use the lesson commentary to fill in gaps in learners' understanding.

### Into Life

Ask learners to brainstorm how the concept of the sacredness of human life is being attacked today; jot responses on the board *(possibilities: abortion, euthanasia, embryonic stem cell research, genocide).* Then ask learners to discuss ways that they can "make a holy noise" on these issues *(possibilities: participate in a March for Life; volunteer at a local senior center; etc.).*

*Option:* Distribute copies of the "A Sacred Promise" activity from the reproducible page. Provide colored pencils to enable learners to create their symbols as directed.

# God Scatters the Nations

**Devotional Reading:** 2 Chronicles 34:22-28
**Background Scripture:** Genesis 11:1-9

## Genesis 11:1-9

**1 And the whole earth was of one language, and of one speech.**

**2 And it came to pass, as they journeyed from the east, that they found a plain in the land of Shinar; and they dwelt there.**

**3 And they said one to another, Go to, let us make brick, and burn them throughly. And they had brick for stone, and slime had they for morter.**

**4 And they said, Go to, let us build us a city and a tower, whose top may reach unto heaven; and let us make us a name, lest we be scattered abroad upon the face of the whole earth.**

**5 And the LORD came down to see the city and the tower, which the children of men builded.**

**6 And the LORD said, Behold, the people is one, and they have all one language; and this they begin to do: and now nothing will be restrained from them, which they have imagined to do.**

**7 Go to, let us go down, and there confound their language, that they may not understand one another's speech.**

**8 So the LORD scattered them abroad from thence upon the face of all the earth: and they left off to build the city.**

**9 Therefore is the name of it called Babel; because the LORD did there confound the language of all the earth: and from thence did the LORD scatter them abroad upon the face of all the earth.**

## Key Verse

*The LORD scattered them abroad from thence upon the face of all the earth: and they left off to build the city.*
**—Genesis 11:8**

Photo: Hemera Technologies / Photos.com / Thinkstock

# First Things

## Unit 1: First Days

Lessons 1–5

## Lesson Aims

After participating in this lesson, each student will be able to:

1. Recount the events surrounding the attempt to construct the Tower of Babel and the Lord's thwarting of that attempt.
2. Tell why the people were wrong in what they were trying to do at Babel and compare that error with similar sins of today.
3. Identify signs that the tower builders' sinful attitude exists in his or her church and suggest a plan for dealing with it.

## Lesson Outline

Introduction
- A. A Tale of Two Towers
- B. Lesson Background

I. The Setting (Genesis 11:1, 2)
- A. One Language (v. 1)
- B. One Location (v. 2)

II. The Scheme (Genesis 11:3, 4)
- A. Resources (v. 3)
- B. Resolution (v. 4)
  - *The Right Kind of Elevation*

III. The Sovereign God (Genesis 11:5-9)
- A. He Sees (v. 5)
- B. He Speaks (vv. 6, 7)
  - *What God Hears*
- C. He Scatters (vv. 8, 9)

Conclusion
- A. Humanity's "Bridges to Nowhere"
- B. God's "Bridge to Somewhere"
- C. Prayer
- D. Thought to Remember

## Introduction

### A. A Tale of Two Towers

John Tower served as a United States senator from Texas for nearly 24 years. After leaving the Senate, Tower continued to be involved in American politics until his death in a plane crash in 1991. In contrast with his last name, John Tower stood only 5'5" tall. "My name is Tower," he would tell people, "but I don't."

Today's text tells about the attempt to build the Tower of Babel—a project undertaken by people who wanted to "tower" over everyone, including God. Because of their misplaced motivation, God brought judgment on them and abruptly halted their efforts. As a result, their tower—didn't.

### B. Lesson Background

Some refer to the first 11 chapters of Genesis as *primeval history.* This means that Genesis 1–11 records events that happened in the earliest ages of history. It should be emphasized that these events are indeed *history*—they are not to be placed in the realm of myth or fiction. Certainly, the testimonies of Jesus and the New Testament writers are crucial here; all of them treat the Old Testament record with the utmost respect and assume the historicity of any event to which they refer. These include events in Genesis 1–11 (see Matthew 24:37-39; Romans 5:12-14; 1 Corinthians 15:45; 2 Corinthians 11:3; and 1 Peter 3:18-20).

Genesis 10, which immediately precedes today's text, includes what is called *the table of nations.* This describes where the families of the sons of Noah settled after the flood. The chapter concludes with this statement: "These are the families of the sons of Noah, after their generations, in their nations: and by these were the nations divided in the earth after the flood" (Genesis 10:32). Verses 5, 20, and 31 reveal more than one language being spoken by these descendants. The account of the Tower of Babel (today's text) tells how this dividing of humanity in terms of languages occurred.

We cannot know with certainty how many years passed between Noah's flood and the point where Genesis 11 begins. Time is not Scripture's primary concern here (which is often true within these early chapters of Genesis). The focus is more on people, especially their relationship with God. That focus lets us see the blessings that accompany obedience and the discipline that accompanies disobedience.

After reading the account of the flood in the previous chapters of Genesis, one is led to ask, "Will people change after such a severe act of judgment? Will anything be different?" Sadly, Noah, who is described in such impressive terms earlier (Genesis 6:9), becomes guilty of drunkenness (9:20, 21). One of his sons reacts to Noah's subsequent nakedness in a disrespectful manner (9:22-27). Thus, even at this point it is clear that while sin has been judged, it has not been eliminated.

## I. The Setting

(Genesis 11:1, 2)

### A. One Language (v. 1)

**1. And the whole earth was of one language, and of one speech.**

This account begins with what appears to be a positive statement. The term *one speech* is literally "the same words" in the Hebrew text. This may indicate that the vocabulary within this common language is understood by all people. Or perhaps it indicates that any dialects or diverse speech patterns at this point are not important enough to affect the ability of people to understand one another.

## HOW TO SAY IT

| | |
|---|---|
| Babel | *Bay*-bul. |
| Babylon | *Bab*-uh-lun. |
| cherubims | *chair*-uh-bims. |
| Eiffel | *Eye*-fuhl. |
| Euphrates | You-*fray*-teez. |
| Hiddekel | *Hid*-eh-kell. |
| Japheth | *Jay*-feth. |
| Pisa | *Pea*-zuh. |
| primeval | pry-*me*-vuhl. |
| Shinar | *Shy*-nar. |
| Tigris | *Tie*-griss. |
| ziggurat | *zig*-oo-rat. |

### B. One Location (v. 2)

**2. And it came to pass, as they journeyed from the east, that they found a plain in the land of Shinar; and they dwelt there.**

As people journey *from the east*, they eventually find an appropriate place to settle down. Shinar is the region around Babylon, located in the broad Tigris-Euphrates valley. The Garden of Eden may have been in this vicinity, since the Tigris and Euphrates Rivers are mentioned in connection with the garden's location. (See Genesis 2:14, where *Hiddekel* is another name for the Tigris River). Thus the people are still in "eastern" territory.

*East* has been very significant in Genesis thus far. The Garden of Eden is described as being "eastward" (Genesis 2:8). After Adam and Eve's sin and expulsion from the garden, the Lord stationed cherubims on the east side of Eden to prevent reentry (3:24). Cain made his home "on the east of Eden" following his murder of Abel (4:16). Thus the direction of east has been associated with ominous developments to this point. The account before us will provide yet another one.

*What Do You Think?*

If offered a chance to relocate (better job, etc.), how do you know if it's God's will to do so?

*Talking Points for Your Discussion*

- Providing for your family
- Opportunities for Christian witness
- Opportunity to be involved with a strong church or to help a struggling one
- Other

## II. The Scheme

(Genesis 11:3, 4)

### A. Resources (v. 3)

**3. And they said one to another, Go to, let us make brick, and burn them throughly. And they had brick for stone, and slime had they for morter.**

After having decided to settle in Shinar, the people determine to build permanent structures in which to live. The phrase *Go to* means something like "Come on."

The bricks to be used for construction have to be burned (or baked)—perhaps in a kiln or oven of some kind. Stone would be cheaper to use since stones do not have to be fabricated as bricks must be. But if no stone quarry is nearby and clay is available, the people will have to adopt a more expensive brick-making process. The fact that they are willing to do so shows their determination.

The word *slime* may be confusing to us at first since we naturally do not connect that term with building materials! It probably refers to bitumen, a tarry substance used as an adhesive or sealant (see also Genesis 14:10; Exodus 2:3). Although this material will serve as a binder between the bricks, it is nothing like our modern cement.

### B. Resolution (v. 4)

**4a. And they said, Go to, let us build us a city and a tower, whose top may reach unto heaven;**

Now the people's goals become more specific and loftier. The tower that is part of the planning should not be thought of in terms of, say, the Leaning Tower of Pisa or the Eiffel Tower. Most likely a tower at this time resembles what is called *a ziggurat.* This is a pyramid-like structure with steps that lead upward to a platform on which may be found an altar or shrine for worship of a particular god.

The height of the structure is thought to bring the worshipper closer to the heavens and thus closer to his or her god or gods. The same thinking is behind the construction of the "high places" often mentioned in the Old Testament (example: Leviticus 26:30). We should note, however, that the text before us does not specifically link this structure to any pagan gods or practices.

#### *The Right Kind of Elevation*

In the fifth century AD, there was a classification of monks known as "pillar saints." They built pillars for themselves, resided on these pillars, and achieved wide acclaim. Perhaps the most famous of these individuals was Simeon Stylites (the word *stylites* itself means "pillar"—think "stylus"), who lived AD 390–459. He started out on a pillar that was about 6 feet high, but gradually increased it until the platform was about 60 feet off the ground.

Many people were attracted to him because of his austerity and holiness. No doubt he was a holy man, but he was also eccentric and a bit bizarre. When insects came and laid their eggs on him, he often would cut himself so worms could feed on his bodily fluids. One time when a worm fell off his arm, Simeon replaced it and exclaimed, "Eat what God has given you!"

Many came to Simeon for spiritual counsel, including rulers and emperors. Because he was suspended between Heaven and earth, people thought him to be closer to Heaven, so obviously his words of counsel would have more spiritual value. Those who began the Tower of Babel also thought they could get closer to Heaven by building a tower. They were unsuccessful, and my guess is that the altitude of Simeon did not help much either. Not too many people today think they can get closer to God by increasing their elevation above the ground. Our problem is more along the lines of elevating our minds. See Daniel 4:29, 30; Romans 12:3; Colossians 2:18; etc. —J. B. N.

**4b. And let us make us a name, lest we be scattered abroad upon the face of the whole earth.**

Now we see the problem with the proposed tower: *let us make us a name* clearly indicates that the people's desire is for self-promotion. God is completely absent from their goals and plans.

*What Do You Think?*

How do people attempt to "make a name" for themselves today? Under what circumstances, if any, can this be a good thing to do?

*Talking Points for Your Discussion*

- Proverbs 3:4; 29:23
- John 3:30
- Romans 12:16
- Galatians 6:4

Second, the people claim that they do not want to be *scattered abroad upon the face of the whole earth.* By making a name for themselves—by constructing a tower and a city that will give them a sense of achievement and a permanent place to live, respectively—the people think they will have no need to move anywhere else. The problem with this thinking is that it seems to reveal defiance of God's mandate to "be fruitful, and multiply, and replenish the earth" (Genesis 1:28; 9:1). Again, it is painfully evident that although sin was judged by the great flood, it has not been eliminated.

## III. The Sovereign God

(Genesis 11:5-9)

### A. He Sees (v. 5)

**5. And the Lord came down to see the city and the tower, which the children of men builded.**

Much as God came "walking in the garden" to confront Adam and Eve (Genesis 3:8), here God is described as coming *down to see* what these builders are up to. The language used is probably an ironic (and darkly humorous) way of pointing out the futility of the people's efforts: here they are desiring to build "a tower, whose top may reach unto heaven" (v. 4), yet the fact that the Lord comes down to observe their vain undertaking reveals that the tower isn't high enough!

The phrase *children of men* may be viewed from a couple of angles. It may describe who these self-important individuals really are: despite their high and haughty aims, they are still "children of men," nothing more. If taken in a literal sense as "sons of Adam," then perhaps the message is that these individuals, who desire to be so independent, are in reality acting no differently from their first ancestor. Adam did not escape the consequences of disobeying God, and neither will these people.

### B. He Speaks (vv. 6, 7)

**6. And the Lord said, Behold, the people is one, and they have all one language; and this they begin to do: and now nothing will be restrained from them, which they have imagined to do.**

The idea of being of "one language, and of one speech" (Genesis 11:1) may appear to be a plus at first since this can promote unity of purpose and cooperation. But the Lord sees the situation quite differently. If the unified people are allowed to engage in such a defiant act of self-important disobedience, then *nothing will be restrained from them, which they have imagined to do.*

This language is similar to the way the Lord described His concern over humanity's having access to the tree of life after the first sin was committed: "Behold, the man is become as one of us, to know good and evil: and now, lest he put forth his hand, and take also of the tree of life, and eat, and live for ever" (Genesis 3:22)—then came eviction from the garden. God was concerned about the consequences of humans in a sinful condition having the potential of living forever in that condition.

The issue is much the same here at Babel: that unrestrained human freedom would have devastating consequences. Unity of purpose may seem an ideal goal, but if that unity is devoid of reverence for God and His authority, then the results will be disastrous. "All things are possible for man," some may arrogantly claim, but history has repeatedly illustrated that these "things" often are the most repulsive, barbaric acts imaginable. We can only wonder how many times God has looked at humanity's so-called "proud achievements" and simply shaken His head in sorrow at what amounts to nothing more than Babel revisited.

*What Do You Think?*

What are some ways we can use our freedom to glorify God?

*Talking Points for Your Discussion*

- Regarding freedom of speech
- Regarding freedom of thought
- Regarding freedom of behavior
- Regarding freedom of movement
- Regarding freedom of association

**7. Go to, let us go down, and there confound their language, that they may not understand one another's speech.**

God couches His counterplan in language similar to what the builders themselves have used. *Go to* was used by the builders in verses 3, 4; here the Lord introduces His intentions in the same way. The people had said *let us* (v. 3); the Lord says the same here. The *us* in the Lord's case is most likely a reference to the Trinity.

God's words *let us* in Genesis 1:26 included granting dominion to humans; now, however, the same words serve to restrict humans' dominion, particularly their self-centered schemes in rebellion against God. God therefore declares that He will confound the people's language so that they can no longer *understand one another's speech.* With conversation stymied, the people's efforts to complete their city and tower will come to nothing.

*What Do You Think?*

What more can you or your church do to bridge language barriers for Christ?

*Talking Points for Your Discussion*

- Concerning those in your community who do not speak English
- Concerning the training of missionaries
- Concerning support for Bible translation efforts
- Other

### *What God Hears*

In the 1994 movie *Nell,* Jodie Foster plays the part of a reclusive girl raised by her mother in the backcountry of the North Carolina hills. The mother had experienced a stroke, leaving her with severely impaired speech. After the mother died, Nell was discovered by the local doctor.

No one could understand Nell's slurred speech at first. Eventually, a researcher discovered that Nell's language was indeed English, but she had learned it from her mother, whose impediment had made Nell's speech virtually unrecognizable. Nell was taken to court to decide whether she should be institutionalized. Both sides argued their cases, then Nell spoke up, to everyone's surprise. The doctor had to interpret for her, but Nell was able to explain her situation, and she was granted her freedom to return to the hills.

Speech is a wonderful gift, a marvelous tool of communication. But when speech is misunderstood, the results can be both frustrating and devastating. We all feel inadequate to speak to God at one time or another. Our speech seems slurred, the right words won't come. It is at such times that we rely on the fact that "the Spirit itself maketh intercession for us with groanings which cannot be uttered" (Romans 8:26). Thank God for that heavenly language! —J. B. N.

### C. He Scatters (vv. 8, 9)

**8. So the Lord scattered them abroad from thence upon the face of all the earth: and they left off to build the city.**

Thus the people who don't want to be scattered (v. 4) are now scattered out of sheer frustration at their inability to live in harmony. The fact that they proceed to move *upon the face of all the earth* puts back in motion God's original intention for humanity. *The city* that had begun with such enthusiasm and fervor remains unfinished.

*What Do You Think?*

What lessons did you learn from a time when God closed a door on an unfinished plan or project?

*Talking Points for Your Discussion*

- A church building project
- A business venture
- A service opportunity
- A family or group event
- A personal goal
- Other

**9. Therefore is the name of it called Babel; because the Lord did there confound the language of all the earth: and from thence did the Lord scatter them abroad upon the face of all the earth.**

There appears to be a twofold play on words here involving the name *Babel.* First, *Babel* means "gate of God" in the language of the ancient Babylonians. But this city hardly lives up to such a presumptuous label! Instead of reaching "unto heaven" (v. 4), the builders have become scattered *upon the face of all the earth.* Instead of making a name for themselves as they originally intended (v. 4), they have become humiliated.

As noted previously, Genesis 10 elaborates on the "scattering" in describing the movements of Noah's three sons (Japheth, Ham, and Shem) and their descendants. At the conclusion of each son's account is the note of division according to "tongues" or languages (vv. 5, 20, 31). Thus the "one language" mentioned at the outset of this lesson becomes many.

The other play on words involves the Hebrew word translated as *confound.* This sounds very much like the name *Babel* and is an apt description of what has occurred as a result of God's intervention. (Of course, English gives us a similarly sounding word, *babble,* which implies confusion or nonsense.) Perhaps the intended lesson of this double meaning is that no matter how one looks at this endeavor, *Babel* means "confusion, failure, and frustration."

## Conclusion

### A. Humanity's "Bridges to Nowhere"

The phrase *bridge to nowhere* was used in the U.S. presidential campaign of 2008 to mock a "pork barrel" project: a bridge to be constructed primarily for the purpose of bringing dollars into a certain congressional district regardless of need for the bridge. An Internet search reveals that at least 11 bridges, primarily in the U.S., have been given this negative label. Sometimes bridges were built with all good intentions, but lack of forethought resulted in an unused or unusable bridge for one reason or another.

Genesis 1–11 records earliest humanity's *bridges to nowhere* in relation to God, and today's lesson sketches one of those. The people intended their tower to bridge the gap between earth and Heaven, but God intervened to ensure that the effort went nowhere. But God didn't just put a stop to faulty plans; He replaced those plans with a better one.

### B. God's "Bridge to Somewhere"

Genesis 1–11 is rich with descriptions of God's actions to put humanity back on the right path. God's path is the path to somewhere important: an eternal, sin-free fellowship with Him. Perhaps you have seen artistic depictions of a canyon with the words "sinful people" on one side and "Holy God" on the other side. The two sides in such depictions are separated by the chasm of sin and death, but the chasm is bridged by the cross of Christ (John 3:16; 5:24; Hebrews 2:14, 15; 1 Peter 2:24; etc.).

Many Bible students have noted how the events that transpired on the Day of Pentecost served to reverse what occurred at Babel. Babel involved a confusion of language. But at Pentecost the gift of tongues (or languages) on those speaking brought about an amazing unity. Each person present could hear proclaimed in his or her native language "the wonderful works of God" (Acts 2:11). Many languages were present at Pentecost, yet God brought about a unity that those at Babel could not achieve because their plans were divorced from God's plans.

Visual for Lesson 5

*Point to this visual as you contrast what happened at Babel with what happened on Pentecost.*

Paul Kissling sees what happened in Jerusalem at Pentecost as a "down payment on the reversal of the curse of Babel." The complete reversal will occur in the new Jerusalem, a place where a unity will be demonstrated that those at Babel could not have imagined. John pictures it for us in Revelation 7:9, 10: "After this I beheld, and, lo, a great multitude, which no man could number, of all nations, and kindreds, and people, and tongues, stood before the throne, . . . and cried with a loud voice, saying, Salvation to our God which sitteth upon the throne, and unto the Lamb."

Babel—and all undertakings similar to it—will be long forgotten.

### C. Prayer

Our Father, we pray for the nations of our world to humble themselves before You. May we set the example as we remember that You resist the proud but give grace unto the humble (James 4:6). In Jesus' name, amen.

### D. Thought to Remember

We can reach Heaven only on God's terms.

# Involvement Learning

*Some of the activities below are also found in the helpful student book,* Adult Bible Class.
*Don't forget to download the free reproducible page from www.standardlesson.com to enhance your lesson!*

## Into the Lesson

Before class, do an Internet search for the tallest buildings in the world. Have some pictures of these on display without identification as learners arrive. Ask learners to identify the buildings.

*Alternative:* Ask learners to name some of the tallest skyscrapers in the world. *(Possible responses: Shanghai World Financial Center, Trump International Hotel and Tower, Empire State Building.)* Say, "Today we will read about the first record of an attempt to build a tall structure and why God was displeased with those who tried to build it."

## Into the Word

*Option:* As a pretest, distribute copies of the "Bringing Order to Confusion" activity from the reproducible page, which you can download. Check answers against the Scripture text. You can use this activity to lead into the next exercise.

Divide the board into four columns. Writing left to right, put *Event / Cause / Effect* as headers for the first three columns. Leave the rightmost column unlabeled for the time being. Then divide learners into four groups and give the following Scripture assignments: Group 1, Genesis 11:1, 2; Group 2, Genesis 11:3, 4; Group 3, Genesis 11:5-7; Group 4, Genesis 11:8, 9. Ask groups to read their verses then identify the event, the possible cause of the event, and the effect of that event. Advise that most of the causes will be inferences rather than concrete evidence from the text.

When groups are ready, call for findings and jot them on the board. Expected and possible responses: *Group 1*—event: found a good place to live together; cause: common language; effect: common purpose, common goals, unity. *Group 2*—event: made bricks, built a city and tower; cause: wanted to achieve own purpose rather than God's; effect: made a name for themselves, maintained solidarity. *Group 3*—event: God came down to see; cause: God read man's heart; effect: God confused their language. *Group 4*—event: people scattered; cause: God wanted to thwart man's plan; effect: God's will prevailed over man's.

Lead the class in discussing each event and its stated or possible causes and effects. Allow learners to defend their inferences concerning causes.

Title the fourth column on the board as *Motives.* Ask, "What was behind the people's desire to build a city with a tower?" Record answers in the fourth column. If someone responds by quoting "let us make us a name" from Genesis 11:4, immediately push deeper by asking, "What does that imply?" *(Possible responses: wanted to exclude God from their plans, were being disobedient to God's command to "replenish the earth.")* Brainstorm modern examples of similar sins.

## Into Life

Say, "It's usually fairly easy to spot the 'mote' in someone else's eye, but if we are going to be the church God has called us to be, then we must make sure we have no 'beams' in our own eyes (see Matthew 7:3-5)." Ask learners to evaluate their church as a body of believers to see if it is guilty of the sins of the people of Babel. (Caution: be sure to make this discussion about the church *as a body,* not mentioning any particular individual; do not allow this to become a gripe session.)

Use the following questions to lead the discussion: 1. Which attitudes of the people of Babel can become a problem when the church engages in a building project, and what can be done to prevent that from happening? 2. Is it possible for a church to become "too big"? Why, or why not?

Conclude with a prayer for God's protection on your church so that wrong attitudes don't develop. Ask for God to give wisdom to your church's leadership. As learners depart, distribute copies of the "My Own Babel" exercise from the reproducible page. This should be a take-home activity since it calls for responses that are very personal.

October 6
Lesson 6

# The Promise of a Future

Devotional Reading: Hebrews 11:8-16
Background Scripture: Genesis 12:1-7; 13; 15; 17:8

## Genesis 15:5-21

5 And he brought him forth abroad, and
said, Look now toward heaven, and tell the
stars, if thou be able to number them: and he
said unto him, So shall thy seed be.
6 And he believed in the LORD; and he
counted it to him for righteousness.
7 And he said unto him, I am the LORD that
brought thee out of Ur of the Chaldees, to give
thee this land to inherit it.
8 And he said, Lord GOD, whereby shall I
know that I shall inherit it?
9 And he said unto him, Take me an heifer
of three years old, and a she goat of three years
old, and a ram of three years old, and a turtle-
dove, and a young pigeon.
10 And he took unto him all these, and
divided them in the midst, and laid each piece
one against another: but the birds divided he
not.
11 And when the fowls came down upon the
carcases, Abram drove them away.
12 And when the sun was going down, a
deep sleep fell upon Abram; and, lo, an horror
of great darkness fell upon him.
13 And he said unto Abram, Know of a surety
that thy seed shall be a stranger in a land that is
not theirs, and shall serve them; and they shall
afflict them four hundred years;
14 And also that nation, whom they shall
serve, will I judge: and afterward shall they
come out with great substance.
15 And thou shalt go to thy fathers in peace;
thou shalt be buried in a good old age.
16 But in the fourth generation they shall
come hither again: for the iniquity of the
Amorites is not yet full.
17 And it came to pass, that, when the sun
went down, and it was dark, behold a smok-
ing furnace, and a burning lamp that passed
between those pieces.
18 In the same day the LORD made a cove-
nant with Abram, saying, Unto thy seed have
I given this land, from the river of Egypt unto
the great river, the river Euphrates:
19 The Kenites, and the Kenizzites, and the
Kadmonites,
20 And the Hittites, and the Perizzites, and
the Rephaims,
21 And the Amorites, and the Canaanites,
and the Girgashites, and the Jebusites.

## Key Verse

*In the same day the LORD made a covenant with Abram, saying, Unto thy seed have I given this land, from the river of Egypt unto the great river, the river Euphrates.* —**Genesis 15:18**

# First Things

## Unit 2: First Nation

Lessons 6–9

## Lesson Aims

After participating in this lesson, each student will be able to:

1. Describe the ways that God confirmed His promises to Abram.

2. Explain the importance of the words *believe* and *covenant* in this lesson.

3. Write a prayer that confesses a weakness in believing God's promises.

## Lesson Outline

Introduction
- A. Unbelievable!
- B. Lesson Background

I. A People in the Future (Genesis 15:5, 6)
- A. Declaration (v. 5)
  - *You, the Star*
- B. Decisions (v. 6)

II. A Possession in the Future (Genesis 15: 7-11)
- A. Purpose and Question (vv. 7, 8)
- B. Command and Response (vv. 9-11)
- C. Situations and Outcomes (vv. 12-16)
  - *Surprising Turnarounds*

III. A Promise to Abram (Genesis 15:17-21)
- A. Covenant Confirmed (v. 17)
- B. Covenant Stated (vv. 18-21)

Conclusion
- A. Standing on the Promises
- B. Prayer
- C. Thought to Remember

## Introduction

### A. Unbelievable!

The word *unbelievable* is a choice word to use in response to an account that has an unexpected outcome. Entering the phrase *unbelievable stories* in an Internet search engine provides examples from war, sports, and other backgrounds.

Consider, for example, "the amazin' Mets" of 1969. The previous year, baseball's New York Mets finished ninth in the 10-team National League. The Mets had come into existence in 1962, and the team had never finished higher than that in its 7-year history. To tell anyone in 1968 that the Mets would win the World Series the following year would have drawn laughter. Yet on October 6, 1969—exactly 44 years ago today—the New York Mets won the National League pennant. The Mets then went on to defeat the Baltimore Orioles in the 1969 World Series. *Unbelievable!*

The lesson for today is about a promise with unbelievable dimensions—that Abram would have descendants and that they would be more than the stars he could see and count.

### B. Lesson Background

After the Tower of Babel event (last week's lesson), the people clustered by language groups and migrated to different areas of the earth (see Genesis 10:5, 20, 31). Cities and civilizations developed. Groups such as the Sumerians and Akkadians became powerful. Their artifacts and clay tablets reveal much about them.

God's redemptive plan, for its part, was moving forward according to His schedule. That plan involved relocating a man named Abram from Ur of the Chaldees (or Kasdim) to the land of Canaan. Several sites are mentioned as possibilities for the location of Ur, but the one that is about 170 miles south of Babylon seems to have the best evidence. Ur was a progressive city that some consider as one of the largest cities of antiquity. Estimates of its population are as high as 65,000. Abram and his family left this thriving commercial area and moved to Haran in northern Mesopotamia. Genesis 11:31 states that Terah (Abram's father) is the one who led in the relocation.

Abram was called to leave Haran after his father died (Genesis 12:1; Acts 7:4), and God gave the seven special promises found in Genesis 12:2, 3. The seventh promise has messianic implications: all the families of the earth would be blessed because of Abram.

So Abram journeyed to Canaan. He built his first altar to the Lord in Canaan when he was at Shechem (Genesis 12:6, 7). It was here that Abram received a promise that this was the land that would be given to his descendants. Famine drove the family to Egypt, and then they returned to Canaan (12:10–13:1). Abram and his nephew, Lot, both prospered, but they had to go their separate ways (13:2-12). Again, God promised the land to Abram (13:14, 15).

The "adventures" that follow in Genesis 14 lead up to God's covenant with Abram in Genesis 15. In the opening verses of Genesis 15, we see Abram assured of the Lord's favor. That assurance includes the promise of a son to become Abram's heir. Abram's name is not changed to *Abraham* until Genesis 17, and that distinction will be maintained in this lesson.

## I. A People in the Future

(Genesis 15:5, 6)

### A. Declaration (v. 5)

**5. And he brought him forth abroad, and said, Look now toward heaven, and tell the stars, if thou be able to number them: and he said unto him, So shall thy seed be.**

This verse continues "the word of the Lord" that Abram is receiving beginning in Genesis 15:4. The fact that Abram is instructed to look toward *the stars* indicates that this communication is taking place at night. To do so, Abram is called out of his tent or place of sleep, perhaps as part of the vision or perhaps in a wakeful state. God has already noted the future of Abram's offspring in Genesis 13:16. That proliferation is restated here in terms of the number of stars.

The estimate of the number of stars visible to the naked eye varies, depending on the time of the night and whether a person is in the northern or southern hemisphere. One study says that the grand total of stars visible to the naked eye is 9,110. A report in 2010 suggested that there are 300 sextillion stars in the universe. For Abram, who does not have a telescope, there is certainly "more here than meets the eye"! The primary point is not a specific number of descendants, however, but that there will be many of them.

*What Do You Think?*

How have God's promises been confirmed for you at different stages of your faith journey?

*Talking Points for Your Discussion*

- In "good" times
- In times of conflict
- In times of hardship
- Other

### *You, the Star*

Recently I spent some time at a cabin in the mountains of New Mexico, at an elevation of 7,300 feet. The nighttime sky was incredible. There were far more stars visible than I am used to seeing. Urban areas, with their "light pollution," cause many stars to be obscured altogether. The difference in a rural setting is amazing!

On a cloudless night in a rural area, one can see the Milky Way stretching from horizon to horizon. The Milky Way, the galaxy within which our solar system is located, is called that because it appears as a milky substance in the heavens. It contains at least 200 billion stars. Those stars were in existence when God said "so shall thy seed be."

We don't know the exact number of stars in the universe, but God does. And if He can know each star by its name (Psalm 147:4), He can certainly count the number of Abraham's descendants and know each of us by name as well. Today, it's spiritual, not physical, descent from Abraham that counts (Luke 3:8; John 8:39-47; Galatians 3:7). Let your light shine!

—J. B. N.

### B. Decisions (v. 6)

**6. And he believed in the Lord; and he counted it to him for righteousness.**

We now see Abram's reaction and the Lord's approval of that reaction. This is the first time that a form of the word *believed* occurs in the Bible. This case involves Abram's trust that God will fulfill what He has said. The importance of this is seen in the fact that this verse is quoted three times in the New Testament: in Romans 4:3; Galatians 3:6; and James 2:23 (compare Romans 4:9, 22; Hebrews 11:8-12).

This is not the first time that faith is demonstrated in the Bible, however. Hebrews 11 notes that Abel, Enoch, and Noah, who preceded Abram, obeyed God in faith. To have faith does not mean discarding reason or believing what you know is not true. As Abram considers the creation and the fact that God can give life and speak into being what did not previously exist (Romans 4:17), then it is reasonable that God can use Abram's "dead" body and the "deadness" of his wife's womb (4:19) to provide a son.

The Lord's response to Abram's faith is to count or credit that faith to him *for righteousness*. The Hebrew word translated *counted it . . . for* occurs over 100 times in the Old Testament, and it is often translated as some form of *think*. If God thinks a person to be righteous, that is what really matters. Abram's faith is the key to his being counted as righteous in the mind of God.

Both Old and New Testaments affirm that no one is righteous in terms of never sinning (Ecclesiastes 7:20; Romans 3:10). Righteousness is not something that a person can earn "by the deeds of the law" (Romans 3:20). But God's gracious provisions mean that He can count a person as righteous. Abram's belief is the basis for that here. Our faith is also a basis (Romans 4:5).

## II. A Possession in the Future

(Genesis 15:7-11)

### A. Purpose and Question (vv. 7, 8)

**7. And he said unto him, I am the Lord that brought thee out of Ur of the Chaldees, to give thee this land to inherit it.**

The Lord leaves no doubt that He is the one who brought Abram *out of Ur of the Chaldees*. The purpose was not just to move Abram away from a certain place, but to bring him to Canaan in order to give him that land as an inheritance. This reaffirms similar statements in Genesis 12. There also are similarities between the verse before us and the opening statement by the Lord as He gives the Ten Commandments to Israel (Exodus 20:2). When God speaks through Moses hundreds of years later, God will affirm that not only is He bringing the people out of slavery in Egypt, but also into the land of promise (see Exodus 13:3-5).

We may wonder what is so special about Canaan that the Lord chooses it for a people, a temple, and the place where the Messiah is to be born. Canaan is the crossroads of the ancient world, lying between Africa and Asia. Commerce to the west, among the nations around the Mediterranean, always thrives. These factors will help spread the concept of "one God" in all directions.

*What Do You Think?*

What helps you trust God when He overrides your plan with one of His own?

*Talking Points for Your Discussion*

- Concerning your church
- Concerning your vocation
- Concerning your family
- Other

**8. And he said, Lord God, whereby shall I know that I shall inherit it?**

At first glance, we may think that Abram's question reveals doubt on his part. The total context, however, indicates that God does not perceive Abram to be expressing skepticism (contrast Luke 1:18-20). Abram does believe, but his question suggests that it would be helpful to have a symbol or sign to confirm the events of the vision. That is about to happen!

### B. Command and Response (vv. 9-11)

**9. And he said unto him, Take me an heifer of three years old, and a she goat of three years old, and a ram of three years old, and a turtledove, and a young pigeon.**

The vision of the night seems to have ended, although some students consider the entire event to be a vision. The statement to Abram seems to involve activities of the day and into the next night. As the new day dawns, Abram receives instructions on gathering five kinds of animals. The fact that the heifer, goat, and ram are to be 3 years old seems to have no special significance. Such animals have reached maturity, and they have a youthful vigor.

**10. And he took unto him all these, and divided them in the midst, and laid each piece one against another: but the birds divided he not.**

Abram complies with God's commands, and his actions show that he understands that these animals are not to be burnt offerings. The ritual about to be described is found also in Jeremiah 34:18, 19, and in the records provided by other nations of that part of the world.

The four-legged animals are cut in half, and the pieces are laid so that the two parts of each animal are placed side by side (juxtaposed). There is a space between the halves, and that space is essential to what is about to take place as verse 17 will make clear. The two birds are not cut apart; it is usually assumed they are laid opposite one other.

**11. And when the fowls came down upon the carcases, Abram drove them away.**

Various kinds of birds are attracted to such a scene, and normally this is God's method of "cleaning up" an ecological problem. This time the situation is different. A sacred, significant ritual is pending, and Abram wants to preserve the animals for the ceremony that is to come. He therefore drives away the intruders so that they will not mutilate the carcasses.

### C. Situations and Outcomes (vv. 12-16)

**12. And when the sun was going down, a deep sleep fell upon Abram; and, lo, an horror of great darkness fell upon him.**

Either in reality or as part of the vision, God moves to bring two things upon Abram: *a deep sleep* that is beyond what is normal (see the commentary on Genesis 2:21 in lesson 2) and a sense of oppressive, *great darkness*. The interpretation is not provided, but it is usually believed that the darkness causes Abram to be aware of the suffering that his descendants will experience (next verse).

**13. And he said unto Abram, Know of a surety that thy seed shall be a stranger in a land that is not theirs, and shall serve them; and they shall afflict them four hundred years.**

The pronouncement by God provides understanding to the oppression that Abram feels. Exodus 12:40, 41 states that the total time spent in Egypt is exactly 430 years. This is not a contradiction to the 400 years noted here, for the Israelites will be protected by Joseph during their early years, and those years may not be counted as part of the centuries of slavery. In addition, large numbers are often rounded (compare Acts 7:6).

**14. And also that nation, whom they shall serve, will I judge: and afterward shall they come out with great substance.**

The name of the oppressing nation is not given, but Egypt is obviously the one that fulfills the prophecy. The judgment that the Lord will declare will be severe indeed (see Exodus 7:14–11:10; 12:29, 30; 14:23-31). God will indeed execute justice on that nation, and then Abram's descendants will leave.

When the Israelites are thrust out of Egypt after the deaths of all firstborn Egyptians, the Israelites will be given things of value (Exodus 12:33-36). In one sense, this too will be justice, for the Israelites finally will be compensated for their hard labor as slaves.

## HOW TO SAY IT

| | |
|---|---|
| Akkadians | Uh-*kay*-dee-unz. |
| Al-'Arish | Awl-A-*reesh*. |
| Amorites | *Am*-uh-rites. |
| Canaanites | *Kay*-nun-ites. |
| Chaldees | *Kal*-deez. |
| Girgashites | *Gur*-guh-shites. |
| Hittites | *Hit*-ites or *Hit*-tites. |
| Hivites | *Hi*-vites. |
| Jebusites | *Jeb*-yuh-sites. |
| Kenites | *Ken*-ites. |
| Mediterranean | *Med*-uh-tuh-***ray***-nee-un. |
| Mesopotamia | *Mes*-uh-puh-***tay***-me-uh. |
| Perizzites | *Pair*-ih-zites. |
| Rephaims | *Ref*-a-ims. |
| Shechem | *Shee*-kem or *Shek*-em. |
| Sumerians | Sue-*mer*-ee-unz. |
| Terah | *Tair*-uh. |

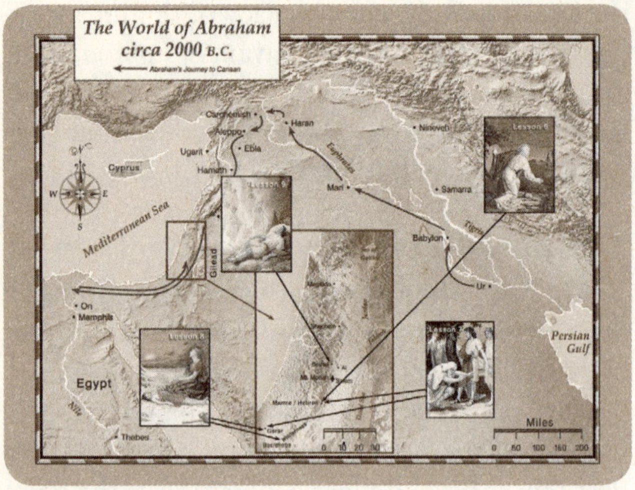

Visual for Lessons 6 & 9. *Keep this visual posted throughout this unit of lessons to give your learners a geographical perspective.*

### *Surprising Turnarounds*

Some time ago, I read a story about a janitor who worked at a small liberal arts college. He never earned a big salary, but he often asked the economics professors about investing. When the janitor died at a ripe old age, he bequeathed the college $3 million from his estate! Here was a man in a "low" position who surprised everyone.

We all like stories like that, don't we? But such stories go back a long way. Abram moved from a center of civilization to endure the hardships (even famine) of a less prosperous area, only to end up very rich (Genesis 13:2). Starting with little more than the shirt on his back, Jacob reversed that trip and ended up wealthy (30:43).

The children of Israel suffered while in Egypt, but ultimately they gained their freedom and left "with great substance." That was a surprising turnaround, but earthly reversals of fortune ultimately are not as important as heavenly ones. The story of the rich man and Lazarus is crucial in this regard (Luke 16:19-31). Make sure you don't allow your earthly circumstances to distract you from the ultimate turnaround that awaits. —J. B. N.

**15. And thou shalt go to thy fathers in peace; thou shalt be buried in a good old age.**

Assurance is given to Abram that he will not experience this enslavement himself. Abram is between 75 and 86 years old at this point (Genesis 12:4; 16:16), and he will be 175 at the time of his death (25:7). He will indeed die "in a good old age, an old man, and full of years" (25:8, 9).

**16. But in the fourth generation they shall come hither again: for the iniquity of the Amorites is not yet full.**

Abram now receives a different time factor: the liberation of his descendants will be *in the fourth generation.* It is thus obvious that a generation is considered to be about 100 years at this time. The longevity of Abram, Isaac, and Jacob—who die at ages 175, 180, and 147, respectively—demonstrates this (Genesis 25:7; 35:28; 47:28).

Another factor is that the present occupants of Canaan, here called *the Amorites,* will also experience divine judgment. The name of one of the largest groups is used to represent all of them (compare Genesis 15:19, 20, below).

*What Do You Think?*

How do you see the faith and actions of past generations bearing fruit in your life today?

*Talking Points for Your Discussion*

- Regarding physical ancestors
- Regarding spiritual ancestors

## III. A Promise to Abram

(Genesis 15:17-21)

### A. Covenant Confirmed (v. 17)

**17. And it came to pass, that, when the sun went down, and it was dark, behold a smoking furnace, and a burning lamp that passed between those pieces.**

The Jeremiah passage cited above with verse 10 shows that this type of covenant requires that the participants walk in the open path between the halves of each animal. According to ancient texts, the implication is that the ones entering into the covenant are making a solemn commitment, and that they will experience death (as represented by the slain animals) if they violate their parts of the covenant. The covenant in view here is known as *a grant covenant*; it does not place any demands on the recipient. God is binding himself to do as He has promised, and Abram is not required to walk between the halves of the animals.

Neither does God personally do any walking. Instead, He uses *a smoking furnace* (a clay oven) and *a burning lamp* to go *between those pieces.* A clay oven is an inverted bowl, probably about two feet high, with a hole near the top that allows a draft to keep the fire burning. The seriousness of this ceremony leaves no doubt: God intends to fulfill His grant.

### B. Covenant Stated (vv. 18-21)

**18. In the same day the LORD made a covenant with Abram, saying, Unto thy seed have I given this land, from the river of Egypt unto the great river, the river Euphrates.**

This verse is significant in that it is the first time that the word *covenant* is used to describe God's promises to Abram. It also provides an answer to the question that Abram asked earlier (v. 8) about an assurance that he will inherit the land.

The promised land is described in two ways. The first description is in terms of geographical points. *The river of Egypt unto the great river, the river Euphrates* describes the range from the southwest to the far north and east. The Egyptian boundary refers to a small stream (the Wadi Al-'Arish) that is recognized as the point where a person enters Egypt when coming from Canaan.

*What Do You Think?*

What will you do to ensure that you are leaving a legacy of faith for future generations?

*Talking Points for Your Discussion*

- Through behavior modeled
- Through evident spiritual disciplines
- Through personal teaching
- Other

**19. The Kenites, and the Kenizzites, and the Kadmonites,**

A second way to describe the promised land is by listing its inhabitants. According to this verse and the next two, there are 10 tribal groups. A comparison with Deuteronomy 7:1 reveals that the Hivites are not mentioned here, but the verse before us adds three not discussed there (compare Exodus 3:8 in lesson 10, which has the same groups as Deuteronomy 7:1, differently ordered).

**20, 21. And the Hittites, and the Perizzites, and the Rephaims, and the Amorites, and the Canaanites, and the Girgashites, and the Jebusites.**

Commentary on Exodus 3:8, 17 in lesson 10 provides a bit more depth on the people groups that inhabit the promised land. The reaction of Abram to these stunning promises is not given. It is assumed that his faith in God is made even stronger by what transpires in the ceremony.

*What Do You Think?*

What obstacles, spiritual and otherwise, will have to be cleared out of the way to enable you to serve God as you should?

*Talking Points for Your Discussion*

- Urgent issues displacing important issues
- Perfectionism
- Procrastination
- Other

## Conclusion

### A. Standing on the Promises

God is a maker of promises! He made promises of land, children, and forgiveness of sin. He also promised consequences for disobedience. The promises began in the Garden of Eden, and they were made through the centuries until the completion of His revelations as recorded in the Bible.

Someone observed that the gospel consists of four things: facts to be believed, commands to be obeyed, promises to be received, and warnings to be heeded. Each factor is important to the believer who is standing on the promises of God. May we exhibit the faith of Abram in believing God's promises—and acting on them.

### B. Prayer

Thank You, Almighty God, for these examples of covenant love and for the promises that You have revealed about the glorious future for all who follow Christ. In Jesus' name, amen.

### C. Thought to Remember

Expect God to keep His promises—
because He will!

# INVOLVEMENT LEARNING

*Some of the activities below are also found in the helpful student book,* Adult Bible Class.
*Don't forget to download the free reproducible page from www.standardlesson.com to enhance your lesson!*

## Into the Lesson

*Option:* Place in chairs copies of the "Abram and Me" activity from the reproducible page, which you can download. Learners can begin working on this as they arrive. Wait until the Into Life segment to discuss results.

As learners arrive, have on display a large clear-glass jar filled with sand. Display next to it a sign reading, "Guess the number, get a prize!" After your class assembles, hold up the jar and say, "We've all seen 'guess the number' contests, often involving jelly beans, marbles, etc. Such contests are easy to determine a winner since it's a simple matter to dump out the jelly beans and count them after the contest deadline. But who would actually want to do that with grains of sand?"

Point out Genesis 15:5. Say, "God tells Abram that his descendants will be as the stars. In 22:17, God adds the illustration of sand. God can count these things, but we need not do so. Our task, as Abram's, is to take God at His word."

## Into the Word

Recruit a volunteer to appear as Abram in Bible-times dress to deliver the following monologue:

> After the great flood and the foolishness of a tower to Heaven—two stories I had heard repeated many times growing up—my ancestor Shem and his descendants settled in a fertile area near two rivers. I was living in the same area, at Haran, when God spoke to me. I do not understand why He spoke to *me,* of all people, regarding His plans! My wife was not able to have children, but God said He would make a great nation of me. After we had journeyed to Canaan, then to Egypt, and then back to Canaan, God spoke once more. He had more startling news: He would give me a son, my own flesh and blood, as an heir! How could I believe such a thing at my age? But I must. For God is true.

After thanking "Abram," let the class comment on both the scriptural and the "poetic license" aspects of the monologue, but do not let this discussion drag out.

Use the commentary to explain the ceremony of Genesis 15:9-17. Then pose the following questions to your class, allowing time for response between each. Some responses will be conjectural since the Scripture references noted do not provide the complete answer in every instance.

1. What question from Abram elicited this ceremony by God? *(v. 8)*
2. Why did Abram drive away the birds of prey? *(v. 11)*
3. What was Abram's state of consciousness during the ceremony? *(v. 12)*
4. What part did God's revelation of the foreign captivity have in assuring Abram of His promise? *(v. 13)*
5. Why was Abram assured that he would live a long life and die in peace? *(v. 15)*
6. How did a listing of the tribal groups occupying Canaan offer assurance to Abram? *(vv. 19-21)*

## Into Life

*Option:* If you used the "Abram and Me" activity above, ask learners what the hidden message is. Use that to make a transition to this segment.

Give each learner a slip of paper that reads "Believing God is not always easy" on one side and "God counts belief as righteousness" on the other. Say, "Keep this slip of paper with you in the week ahead. Before you pray at various times, first read both sides of the paper. Then relate the two truths on the paper for the issue of prayer that is presenting itself at the time."

*Alternative:* Distribute copies of the "The Desperate Father and Me" activity from the reproducible page. Have someone read aloud Mark 9:17-26. Discuss the mixture of belief and unbelief that is honestly confessed in verse 24; have learners fill in the blanks per instructions and exchange results with someone. Close with a prayer for belief.

# A Promise to Sarah

**Devotional Reading:** Isaiah 51:1-6
**Background Scripture:** Genesis 17:15-17; 18:9-15; 21:1-7

## Genesis 17:15-17

15 And God said unto Abraham, As for Sarai thy wife, thou shalt not call her name Sarai, but Sarah shall her name be.

16 And I will bless her, and give thee a son also of her: yea, I will bless her, and she shall be a mother of nations; kings of people shall be of her.

17 Then Abraham fell upon his face, and laughed, and said in his heart, Shall a child be born unto him that is an hundred years old? and shall Sarah, that is ninety years old, bear?

## Genesis 18:9-15

9 And they said unto him, Where is Sarah thy wife? And he said, Behold, in the tent.

10 And he said, I will certainly return unto thee according to the time of life; and, lo, Sarah thy wife shall have a son. And Sarah heard it in the tent door, which was behind him.

11 Now Abraham and Sarah were old and well stricken in age; and it ceased to be with Sarah after the manner of women.

12 Therefore Sarah laughed within herself, saying, After I am waxed old shall I have pleasure, my lord being old also?

13 And the LORD said unto Abraham, Wherefore did Sarah laugh, saying, Shall I of a surety bear a child, which am old?

14 Is any thing too hard for the LORD? At the time appointed I will return unto thee, according to the time of life, and Sarah shall have a son.

15 Then Sarah denied, saying, I laughed not; for she was afraid. And he said, Nay; but thou didst laugh.

## Genesis 21:1-7

1 And the LORD visited Sarah as he had said, and the LORD did unto Sarah as he had spoken.

2 For Sarah conceived, and bare Abraham a son in his old age, at the set time of which God had spoken to him.

3 And Abraham called the name of his son that was born unto him, whom Sarah bare to him, Isaac.

4 And Abraham circumcised his son Isaac being eight days old, as God had commanded him.

5 And Abraham was an hundred years old, when his son Isaac was born unto him.

6 And Sarah said, God hath made me to laugh, so that all that hear will laugh with me.

7 And she said, Who would have said unto Abraham, that Sarah should have given children suck? for I have born him a son in his old age.

## Key Verse

*Sarah conceived, and bare Abraham a son in his old age, at the set time of which God had spoken to him.*

**—Genesis 21:2**

# First Things

## Unit 2: First Nation

Lessons 6–9

## Lesson Aims

After participating in this lesson, each student will be able to:

1. Describe the reactions of Abraham and Sarah to the promise of a son.
2. Explain the significance of laughing in each section of today's text.
3. Suggest a way to show God that he or she trusts God's plans.

## Lesson Outline



## Introduction

### A. Making Promises

The investors had to promise that they would not tell anyone about the project, which was top secret. Anyone who violated this nondisclosure agreement would forfeit his or her investment. The supposed project involved a method of producing energy so that a unit the size of a small box could provide electricity for a city.

If this sounds too good to be true, it was. Those who received the funds for the imaginary project were master manipulators. They spent the money on themselves, declared bankruptcy, and depended on the investors to keep their promises not to spill the beans. Someone, however, finally talked. Did he lose what he invested? Yes—and so did the ones who kept the promise.

Some people make promises to God that are intended to manipulate God into doing what they want. The phrase *foxhole religion* describes another category of suspect promises. The one making this type of promise commits his or her future, with all sincerity, to God if God will only spare the person from imminent danger. But the promise may fade from memory once the danger has passed.

Today's lesson is about promises that God made to Sarah about her having a son. God's promises are not like ours—He never manipulates; His memory doesn't fade. When God promises, He keeps His word, and we receive the benefits.

### B. Lesson Background

God made several promises to Abram. When Abram's family left Haran, the Lord said that He would make Abram to be a great nation (Genesis 12:2). Abram entered Canaan at age 75, and he was told that this was the land that God planned to give to his descendants (12:7). After Abram and nephew Lot went their separate ways, Abram was again told that all the land he could see would be given to his descendants (13:15).

But Abram and his wife were childless. With the passing of the years, Abram may have been thinking again how he could "help" God resolve this problem of Abram's having a proper heir. In Genesis 16, Abram's wife, Sarai (renamed Sarah in today's lesson), offered a culturally acceptable way that could fulfill what had been promised: she would give Hagar, her maidservant, to Abram. The resulting offspring would be from Abram's body, and Sarai could have a son through Hagar. This attempt to run ahead of God turned out to be a bad idea, as Genesis 16:4b-6 shows.

The Lord appeared to Abram 13 years later to reveal new dimensions of the covenant (Genesis 17:1). First, Abram's name (meaning "exalted father") was changed to Abraham (meaning "father of a multitude"; 17:5). It was strange for a man who had only one son (Ishmael) to have such a name! Even so, Abraham's acceptance of the name shows that he understood that to change a person's name shows that you have authority over that person. Today's text takes us into a second name change initiated by the authority of God.

## I. Prediction

(Genesis 17:15-17)

Between God's changing of Abram's name (Genesis 17:3-5) and the changing of Sarai's name (today's text) comes the Lord's introduction of the practice of circumcision for all males who are in Abraham's household. This is a sign of the covenant (v. 11).

The seriousness of God's intent is seen in His declaration that failure to undergo circumcision is the same as breaking the covenant (v. 14). Abraham's two parts of the covenant are to understand it (vv. 1-14) and implement it (vv. 23-27). Sandwiched between these two is God's declaration of Sarai's role.

## HOW TO SAY IT

| | |
|---|---|
| Abraham | *Ay*-bruh-ham. |
| Abram | *Ay*-brum. |
| Hagar | *Hay*-gar. |
| Ishmael | *Ish*-may-el. |
| Keturah | Keh-*too*-ruh. |
| Mamre | *Mam*-reh. |
| Sarai | *Seh*-rye. |
| Yahweh *(Hebrew)* | *Yah*-weh. |
| Zacharias | Zack-uh-*rye*-us. |

### A. Name Given (v. 15)

**15. And God said unto Abraham, As for Sarai thy wife, thou shalt not call her name Sarai, but Sarah shall her name be.**

Abraham's wife, Sarai, has not been mentioned in any previous communications from God regarding Abraham's having a son, so this section of Scripture is a first in that regard (see v. 16, next). Just before that happens, she is mentioned as another person whose name is being changed. This time, however, there is no difference in meaning: both *Sarah* and *Sarai* mean "princess." An example of this meaning is found in 1 Kings 11:3, where it is given in the plural form as "princesses."

Some suggest that the minor change in the name may be a difference in dialect. The unchanged meaning fits Sarah's forthcoming status, as verse 16 reveals.

#### *Your New Name*

Fans of professional wrestling know that Terrance Gene Bollea gained fame on TV under a different name. In another case, Angelo Siciliano, the bodybuilder of the 1940s, marketed his system for muscle development by giving himself a name that created a mental image of success in that regard. If you're a baseball fan of any era, you probably know the nickname by which George Herman Ruth, Jr. was called.

Did the three well-known substitute names come to mind? They are Hulk Hogan, Charles Atlas, and Babe Ruth, respectively. Hogan's professional moniker added to his cachet as a TV personality, while Siciliano's new name conjured up visions of a Titan from Greek mythology. Both changes were successful in terms of marketing. Ruth's nickname is a bit different because he didn't choose the new name for himself; rather, it was imposed upon him by teammates and fans.

We see several name changes in the Bible, and Sarah's is one of those. She didn't choose her new name, God did. The new name had the same meaning as the old one, but the change symbolized the authority and power God had over her life. This is a marvelous thing because "him that overcometh . . . I will write upon him my new name" (Revelation 3:12). —C. R. B.

*What Do You Think?*

What name would you pick for yourself to describe the spiritual reality of your life? Why?

*Talking Points for Your Discussion*

- Name of a Bible character
- Name of a Bible story
- Name drawn from a life-changing event
- Other

### B. Son Promised (v. 16)

**16. And I will bless her, and give thee a son also of her: yea, I will bless her, and she shall be a mother of nations; kings of people shall be of her.**

Sarah is to be the mother of the special son promised to Abraham. For this to happen at her advanced age (see v. 17, next), she will need a blessing from the Lord, and that is what He provides.

The blessing for Abraham and Sarah reaches into the future and includes kings and royalty among their descendants. Thus it is quite appropriate for Sarah's changed name still to mean "princess." The fulfillment for this aspect of the promise begins when Saul becomes Israel's first genuine king more than 1,000 years later. The final king in the long line is Jesus Christ, the "King of kings" (Revelation 17:14).

### C. Father Laughs (v. 17)

**17. Then Abraham fell upon his face, and laughed, and said in his heart, Shall a child be born unto him that is an hundred years old? and shall Sarah, that is ninety years old, bear?**

Abraham's reaction is to fall to the ground in laughter. Some have said that this reflects skepticism, similar to Sarah's in Genesis 18. This negative view doesn't fit the man who looked at the stars of the heavens and believed God (Genesis 15:6). We conclude that Abraham combines an attitude of worship with laughter that results from an inner joy (compare Romans 4:19-21).

When Abraham looks ahead, he realizes that at the time of the birth he will be 100 years old and Sarah will be 90 (compare Genesis 17:1, 24). These facts cause him to ask himself the two questions we see here. The implications are staggering, and Abraham knows that the promised outcome is beyond what is considered normal.

Genesis 17:19 (not in today's text) should also be mentioned, for there God informs Abraham that the name of the son is to be *Isaac.* The name means "he laughs," and it points to the laughter here and to what occurs in the next section of our study.

## II. Promise

(Genesis 18:9-15)

The opening verses of Genesis 18 provide the background for the dialogue that is a part of the printed text for today. Abraham is near Mamre, and three men are suddenly standing in front of him (see Hebrews 13:2). This probably takes place a short time after the first segment of our lesson.

To have guests show up is special, for they can bring news from far away. Therefore Abraham instructs Sarah and a servant to prepare a meal of hospitality (Genesis 18:6, 7). The men ask the questions we see next.

### A. Listening and Laughing (vv. 9-12)

**9. And they said unto him, Where is Sarah thy wife? And he said, Behold, in the tent.**

In the culture of the day, it is not customary for a man to inquire about the wife of another man. Therefore Abraham is probably curious about the inquiry we see here. Perhaps there is something about these men that causes Abraham to accept the question, so he replies that she is *in the tent.*

**10. And he said, I will certainly return unto thee according to the time of life; and, lo, Sarah thy wife shall have a son. And Sarah heard it in the tent door, which was behind him.**

One of the guests speaks, and in so doing he states that he will return later. Opinions vary on the figure of speech *according to the time of life* used to describe when the return will occur. One view is that it will be at the beginning of another year from the present moment. Another opinion is that it will be when the dormancy of winter is changing to the new life of spring. Romans 9:9 offers the translation "at this time will I come," but this doesn't help much in pointing to one interpretation over the other. Genesis 18:1 implies that this conversation takes place in the heat of summer, so the interpretations of the timing of the promised return vary by only a few months in any case.

As the special guest continues, Sarah has positioned herself on the other side of the tent flap, directly behind the one who is speaking. What she overhears is a shocking statement to one of her age, for the man announces that at the time of his return she will *have a son*.

**11. Now Abraham and Sarah were old and well stricken in age; and it ceased to be with Sarah after the manner of women.**

At this point, Abraham is 99 and Sarah is 89 years of age (compare Genesis 17:17, above). Sarah's age means that she is no longer experiencing the monthly cycle that is associated with the ability to conceive children. We may compare the life situation of these two with that of Zacharias and Elisabeth in Luke 1:5-7.

*What Do You Think?*

How have you seen God work through someone in a way not usually associated with his or her stage of life? How has this increased your faith?

*Talking Points for Your Discussion*

- Through a child
- Through a teenager
- Through an elderly person

**12. Therefore Sarah laughed within herself, saying, After I am waxed old shall I have pleasure, my lord being old also?**

Sarah quickly evaluates the announcement by the stranger to be preposterous, and this prompts a silent laughter *within herself.* To burst forth in laughter would reveal that she is eavesdropping on the conversation of the men.

Sarah is fully aware that both she and her husband are *waxed old.* To her, it is quite unreasonable to think that she can conceive and bear a child (compare Romans 4:17, 19). Therefore both Abraham's laughter of delight and the laughter of Sarah's doubt are reflected in the name of their son to be born (see the commentary on 17:17).

At some point, Sarah's doubt gives way to faith since Hebrews 11:11 says, "Through faith also Sara herself received strength to conceive seed, and was delivered of a child when she was past age, because she judged him faithful who had promised."

*What Do You Think?*

What helps you overcome doubt that threatens your trust in God's promises?

*Talking Points for Your Discussion*

- When events seem to contradict God's promises
- When God seems to be doing nothing
- When people around you are giving in to doubt
- Other

### B. Response and Reaction (vv. 13-15)

**13. And the LORD said unto Abraham, Wherefore did Sarah laugh, saying, Shall I of a surety bear a child, which am old?**

The most important fact of this verse is that the speaker is now designated as *the Lord.* When the four letters of this word are all capital letters, it indicates that this is the divine name *Yahweh.* The three guests were earlier called "men" (Genesis 18:2), and Hebrews 13:2 uses the term "angels." The word *angel* can mean "messenger," and that is the situation here. The speaker is the Lord himself, and He is the special messenger from Heaven.

Some scholars believe that this is a manifestation of God the Son before He is born as a babe in Bethlehem. The special nature of this messenger is seen in the bold pronouncement and in being able to know the unexpressed thoughts and silent laughter of Sarah.

**14. Is any thing too hard for the LORD? At the time appointed I will return unto thee, according to the time of life, and Sarah shall have a son.**

The Lord's responses continue with a rhetorical question and an affirmation. The thrust of the question *Is any thing too hard for the Lord?* is repeated in different circumstances in both the Old and New Testaments. As a question, we see it in Jeremiah 32:27. As a statement, we see it in Jeremiah 32:17; Matthew 19:26; Luke 1:37; and Romans 4:21. The difficult statement *I will return unto thee, according to the time of life* is identical in Hebrew to the one found in Genesis 18:10 (above), except for the added word *certainly* there.

**15. Then Sarah denied, saying, I laughed not; for she was afraid. And he said, Nay; but thou didst laugh.**

Sarah reacts with a feeble attempt to defend herself. Perhaps she rationalizes that there has been no audible laughter, but God knows a person's heart and thoughts (compare Matthew 9:4; 12:25).

## III. Fulfillment

(Genesis 21:1-7)

We may assume that Sarah's unusual pregnancy runs the usual nine months in duration. During this time Lot and his daughters are rescued from catastrophe (Genesis 19), and Abraham repeats a cowardly act (compare Genesis 20 with 12:10-20).

### A. Birth of the Son (vv. 1, 2)

**1. And the Lord visited Sarah as he had said, and the Lord did unto Sarah as he had spoken.**

The first verse of Genesis 21 is a general statement that is intended to show that the Lord keeps His promises to Sarah. Although not recorded, Sarah's laughter of disbelief probably turns into a laughter of joy during her pregnancy. We would like to know more about such things (compare Genesis 25:22; Luke 1:41).

*What Do You Think?*

How has reaching a dream or goal later in life than you planned influenced your faith walk?

*Talking Points for Your Discussion*

- Regarding marriage
- Regarding children
- Regarding a financial goal
- Regarding an education goal
- Other

**2. For Sarah conceived, and bare Abraham a son in his old age, at the set time of which God had spoken to him.**

The general statement of verse 1 is followed by a summary of the basic facts surrounding the conception and birth of the child of Abraham and Sarah. It has been 25 years since God first made a promise to Abraham that involved his becoming a great nation (Genesis 12:2), but God's plans are fulfilled at the scheduled time (compare Galatians 4:4).

### B. Naming the Son (vv. 3, 4)

**3. And Abraham called the name of his son that was born unto him, whom Sarah bare to him, Isaac.**

Abraham follows the stipulations and revelations of the God-given covenant. The name given to the son is therefore Isaac (meaning "he laughs"), just as God had said (Genesis 17:19). This name serves as a constant reminder to the parents of the different types of laughter that Abraham and Sarah expressed in their reactions to the promises of God. The lineage of Jesus continues to move forward (Matthew 1:2; Luke 3:34).

**4. And Abraham circumcised his son Isaac being eight days old, as God had commanded him.**

The ritual of circumcision as a sign of the covenant was introduced a year earlier, when Abraham was 99 years old (Genesis 17:10-14, 24). The practice is now applied to the covenantal son of Abraham (Genesis 17:19; Acts 7:8) when the infant is *eight days old,* just *as God had commanded.* Devout Jews of the New Testament era are careful to continue obedience to this command (see Luke 1:59; 2:21; Philippians 3:5).

### C. Parents of the Son (vv. 5-7)

**5. And Abraham was an hundred years old, when his son Isaac was born unto him.**

The factor of Abraham's age is important. It is one way of showing that what has transpired has been through divine intervention. To establish a time line of Abraham's life from the point of his call (as Abram) to his death, see Genesis 12:4; 16:3, 16; 17:1, 17, 24; 21:5; 25:7.

**6, 7. And Sarah said, God hath made me to laugh, so that all that hear will laugh with me. And she said, Who would have said unto Abraham, that Sarah should have given children suck? for I have born him a son in his old age.**

Sarah, age 90, now speaks of the joy that has come into her life with the birth of a son. We can presume that this joy stays with her for the remaining 37 years of her life (Genesis 23:1).

The word *laugh* carries a special meaning for Sarah. A form of it is the name of her son, and she is confident that others will laugh when they learn that God has granted her a son. The promises of God about Sarah's having a son are fulfilled, and that is a source of shared joy. A key part of this joy is the relief at having the stigma of barrenness removed (compare 1 Samuel 1:1–2:11; Psalm 113:9; Luke 1:25).

*What Do You Think?*

What things have you seen that confirm for you that nothing is impossible with God?

*Talking Points for Your Discussion*

- Spiritual issues in your own life
- Spiritual issues in the lives of others
- Relational issues in your own life
- Relational issues in the lives of others
- Other

### *Rhetorical Questions*

In Shakespeare's *The Merchant of Venice,* the Jewish character Shylock asks, "Hath not a Jew eyes? Hath not a Jew hands, organs, dimensions, senses, affections, passions? . . . If you prick us, do we not bleed?" Shylock asks rhetorical questions —questions spoken not to seek information, but to make a point that should be self-evident.

Occasionally, rhetorical questions are used to sell products. A TV ad for Dial® soap in the 1960s asked, "Aren't you glad you use Dial? Don't you wish everybody did?" Other rhetorical questions are intended to amuse. For example, you may have seen this one: "If lawyers are disbarred and clergymen defrocked, doesn't it follow that electricians can be delighted, musicians denoted, cowboys deranged, models deposed, tree surgeons debarked, and dry cleaners depressed?"

We have seen a series of rhetorical questions in today's study, concluding with the one in Genesis 21:7. The obvious answer to "Who would have said unto Abraham, that Sarah should have given children suck?" is *no one!* Joyous Sarah then exults, "I have borne him a son in his old age!" This calls for another question: Is there anything too difficult for God? Well, is there? —C. R. B.

## Conclusion

### A. Abraham's Children

Ishmael, Isaac, . . . and the list of Abraham's descendants continues beyond that. It includes the sons born to Keturah, whom Abraham married after Sarah died (Genesis 25:1, 2; 1 Chronicles 1:32). The list features Jacob, his 12 sons, and many others who became part of the nation of Israel. Romans 4:16 says that Abraham is the father of all who believe. The popular children's chorus of a few years ago was correct when it stated that Father Abraham has many sons; that is great doctrine.

Our belief includes intellectual assent, but it is more than that. These lessons from Genesis are not just to be discussed academically. They should help us develop a stronger, deeper faith in God and give us a blessed assurance that the promises He has made about the future will come to pass. Just look at what God did for Abraham and Sarah!

### B. Prayer

Father in Heaven, thank You for making it possible for me to be one of Your children. May my life be an instrument to lead others to become Your children as well. In Jesus' name, amen.

### C. Thought to Remember

Nothing is too difficult for the Lord.
Nothing.

Visual for Lesson 7. *Point to this visual as you have Jeremiah 32:17, 27; Matthew 19:26; Luke 1:37; and Romans 4:21 read aloud. Discuss.*

# Involvement Learning

*Some of the activities below are also found in the helpful student book,* Adult Bible Class. *Don't forget to download the free reproducible page from www.standardlesson.com to enhance your lesson!*

### Into the Lesson

Have on display a banner reading *A Time to Laugh.* (An artistic class member might enjoy preparing this.) If available, play as class begins a sound track of people laughing. (You can download such a sound track from the Internet, or you can record your own family and friends laughing.)

*Alternative:* Distribute copies of the "What Makes It Funny?" activity from the reproducible page, which you can download. Use this to start a whole-class discussion on the idea of laughter, according to the instructions.

Say, "Laughter may or may not always be appropriate. As we take a closer look at today's text, we'll see what prompted the laughter of Abraham and Sarah and whether or not their laughter was appropriate."

### Into the Word

Ask three volunteers to read aloud today's texts of Genesis 17:15-17; 18:9-15; and 21:1-7, one section each.

In light of the fact that several questions appear in today's text, use the format of the TV show *Jeopardy* to give answers to which learners must ask the questions that go with them. Possible answers and expected questions are as follows. You may wish to show answers on small posters rather than simply reading them.

1. One hundred years old. *What was Abraham's age when Isaac was born? (17:17; 21:5)*
2. Ninety years old. *What was Sarah's age when Isaac was born? (17:17)*
3. This person denied having laughed. *Who was Sarah? (18:15)*
4. This person fell to the ground in laughter. *Who was Abraham? (17:17)*
5. She was formerly known as Sarai. *Who was Sarah? (17:15)*
6. He mentioned Sarah's laughter to Abraham. *Who was the Lord? (18:13)*
7. He was eight days old when circumcised. *Who was Isaac? (21:4)*
8. This person predicted laughter by others. *Who was Sarah? (21:6)*
9. This is mentioned either 7 or 10 times. *What is a form of the word* laugh*? (mentioned 7 times, in 17:17; 18:12, 13, 15; and 21:6, but since the name* Isaac *means "laughter," one might add 3 more per 21:3, 4, 5)*

Divide your class into two segments called *The Abraham Side* and *The Sarah Side.* Say, "Play the part of a prosecutor as you make a case for the laughter of your 'defendant' (Abraham or Sarah) to have reflected lack of faith." Let sides offer their arguments. Use the commentary to support and challenge the arguments. (*Option:* Let each segment challenge the arguments of the other.)

Ask three learners to take turns reading the verses of Romans 4:16-25 aloud. Note that a key idea is God's ability to give life to the dead. This ability extends not only to the "dead" reproductive organs of Abraham and Sarah, but also to God's Son (who was dead in the tomb) and to people dead in sin!

### Into Life

Say, "The Romans 4 passage affirms that Abraham was fully persuaded that God was able to do what He promised (see v. 21)." Give each learner a slip of paper with this commitment statement: "I fully believe that God is able to do what He promises, and I will demonstrate that confidence by ________________ this week." Challenge learners to use the slip as a Bible bookmark for a time and to complete the statement only when they have considered an appropriate response.

*Option:* Distribute copies of the "Believing God" activity from the reproducible page. Have learners complete this in small groups and discuss. This will provide an additional opportunity to carry the truth of the study into daily living.

# Blessings for Ishmael and Isaac

**Devotional Reading:** Hebrews 11:17-22
**Background Scripture:** Genesis 15–17; 21:9-21; 26:1-25

## Genesis 21:12-14, 17-21

**12 And God said unto Abraham, Let it not be grievous in thy sight because of the lad, and because of thy bondwoman; in all that Sarah hath said unto thee, hearken unto her voice; for in Isaac shall thy seed be called.**

**13 And also of the son of the bondwoman will I make a nation, because he is thy seed.**

**14 And Abraham rose up early in the morning, and took bread, and a bottle of water, and gave it unto Hagar, putting it on her shoulder, and the child, and sent her away: and she departed, and wandered in the wilderness of Beersheba.**

. . . . . . . . . . . . . . . . . . . . . . . . . .

**17 And God heard the voice of the lad; and the angel of God called Hagar out of heaven, and said unto her, What aileth thee, Hagar? fear not; for God hath heard the voice of the lad where he is.**

**18 Arise, lift up the lad, and hold him in thine hand; for I will make him a great nation.**

**19 And God opened her eyes, and she saw a well of water; and she went, and filled the bottle with water, and gave the lad drink.**

**20 And God was with the lad; and he grew, and dwelt in the wilderness, and became an archer.**

**21 And he dwelt in the wilderness of Paran: and his mother took him a wife out of the land of Egypt.**

## Genesis 26:2-5, 12, 13

**2 And the Lord appeared unto him, and said, Go not down into Egypt; dwell in the land which I shall tell thee of:**

**3 Sojourn in this land, and I will be with thee, and will bless thee; for unto thee, and unto thy seed, I will give all these countries, and I will perform the oath which I sware unto Abraham thy father;**

**4 And I will make thy seed to multiply as the stars of heaven, and will give unto thy seed all these countries; and in thy seed shall all the nations of the earth be blessed;**

**5 Because that Abraham obeyed my voice, and kept my charge, my commandments, my statutes, and my laws.**

. . . . . . . . . . . . . . . . . . . . . . . . . .

**12 Then Isaac sowed in that land, and received in the same year an hundredfold: and the Lord blessed him.**

**13 And the man waxed great, and went forward, and grew until he became very great.**

## Key Verse

*God said unto Abraham, . . . In Isaac shall thy seed be called. And also of the son of the bondwoman will I make a nation, because he is thy seed.* —**Genesis 21:12, 13**

# First Things

## Unit 2: First Nation

Lessons 6–9

## Lesson Aims

After participating in this lesson, each student will be able to:

1. Describe God's separate blessings on Isaac and Ishmael.

2. Explain the superior blessing of Isaac over that of Ishmael even though Ishmael was born first.

3. Suggest a means of sharing one's faith in Christ with a Muslim.

## Lesson Outline

Introduction
- A. Moses Easterly Lard
- B. Lesson Background

I. Promises for Ishmael (Genesis 21:12-14, 17-21)
- A. Intervention (vv. 12, 13)
- B. Dismissal (v. 14)
  - *The Danger of Impatience*
- C. Assurance (vv. 17, 18)
- D. Development (vv. 19-21)

II. Blessings for Isaac (Genesis 26:2-5, 12, 13)
- A. Promises (vv. 2, 3)
  - *Toward Greener Grass?*
- B. Posterity (vv. 4, 5)
- C. Prosperity (vv. 12, 13)

Conclusion
- A. It's Not a License!
- B. Prayer
- C. Thought to Remember

## Introduction

### A. Moses Easterly Lard

Mary Lard was the mother of six. Her husband had moved the family to western Missouri, but his death from smallpox in about 1829 left her to rear the children alone. In 1830, she made one of the most heart-wrenching decisions that a mother can make. Deciding that there was no way she could feed six children, she told the two oldest sons that they would have to leave. She gave each a small New Testament and bid her farewells with quivering lips. As the boys walked away, they heard their mother scream, a sound they never forgot.

The boy named Moses never told what happened during the next few years. Did the two live off the land, steal, or work for others, perhaps living in barns or caves? Moses Lard had another problem: he could not read. He became an apprentice to a tailor and taught himself to read during that time. He would take letters from signs, put them together in different ways, and ask people about the sounds or the words that resulted.

Moses Lard eventually began to preach, and he caught the attention of Alexander Doniphan, later to be a hero of the Mexican-American War (1846–1848). That man made arrangements for Lard to attend college. Lard graduated in 1849, age 30, as the valedictorian of the class, in spite of having to work to support his family. Lard's ministries included preaching, writing a commentary on the book of Romans, and being a debater and an editor. That's "not bad" for one who had to teach himself to read!

Today's lesson offers certain parallels in that it involves a decision to break up a family because circumstances seemed to require it. Even so, troubling family circumstances can yield good outcomes (Genesis 17:20; 25:12-18).

### B. Lesson Background

Only four verses separate last week's lesson from this one. Since the backgrounds are therefore the same, the Lesson Background of last week need not be repeated here. Instead, we will pay some attention to the literary method that Moses used in writing the book of Genesis.

The first part of the book of Genesis is *general history* (what we also called *primeval history* in lesson 5). As Moses introduces new people or nations throughout this section, the emphasis very quickly moves to the person or entity that he intends to feature at that point. For example, Genesis 1:1 refers to the heavens and earth, but the next verse focuses immediately on the earth. Genesis 2 sharpens the focus to the first humans. The accounts of the first sin and the first murder are set forth in Genesis 3 and 4, but the goal is to get to another son of Adam and Eve—namely, Seth. Notice the focus on him in Genesis 5:1-3. In Genesis 5:6-26, we see repeatedly that a certain descendant "begat sons and daughters," but the only one mentioned by name in each case is the one leading to Noah and the flood.

After the flood, the biblical record gives information about the descendants of Noah's three sons—Shem, Ham, and Japheth (Genesis 9:18, 19). There are 70 founders of nations or people groups mentioned in the table of nations in Genesis 10. The incident of the Tower of Babel (lesson 5) provides an explanation for the presence of different languages among the peoples of the world. After that, the emphasis quickly returns to Shem and his descendants (Genesis 11:10-26). The plan seems to be to move as quickly as possible to Abram, a son of Terah.

The second part of the book of Genesis could be called *personal history.* It is about people who have purpose in the plan of God to bring the Messiah into the world at just the right time (Galatians 4:4). This section of Genesis begins with Genesis 11:27. The focus is on the descendants of Abram that continue through Isaac, Jacob, and the latter's 12 sons. Others are mentioned as they take their places on the stage of history. In this light, the goal for Moses, the author, is to provide an explanation on how the nation of Israel came into existence.

## HOW TO SAY IT

| | |
|---|---|
| Beersheba | Beer-*she*-buh. |
| Gerar | *Gear*-rar (G as in get). |
| Hagar | *Hay*-gar. |
| Haran | *Hair*-un. |
| Isaac | *Eye*-zuk. |
| Ishmael | *Ish*-may-el. |
| Japheth | *Jay*-feth. |
| Nahor | *Nay*-hor. |
| Paran | *Pair*-un. |
| patriarchs | *pay*-tree-arks. |
| primeval | pry-*me*-vuhl. |
| Sinai | *Sigh*-nye or *Sigh*-nay-eye. |
| Terah | *Tair*-uh. |

## I. Promises for Ishmael

(Genesis 21:12-14, 17-21)

Children are weaned between the ages of 2 and 3. The weaning of Isaac when he reaches this age becomes the basis of "a great feast" for the family of Abraham (Genesis 21:8). Big brother Ishmael is age 16 or 17 (see 17:24, 25; 21:5), and for some reason he begins to mock little Isaac (21:9). Sarah, a protective mother of Isaac, her only son, demands that her husband expel Hagar and her son from the household (21:10). Abraham is reluctant to do so because Ishmael is his son (21:11). It is at this point that God intervenes.

### A. Intervention (vv. 12, 13)

**12. And God said unto Abraham, Let it not be grievous in thy sight because of the lad, and because of thy bondwoman; in all that Sarah hath said unto thee, hearken unto her voice; for in Isaac shall thy seed be called.**

Abraham has genuine concerns for Hagar, who is the *bondwoman* or slave, and Ishmael (*the lad,* son of Abraham and Hagar). It is also possible that Abraham is influenced by the customs of the time that make it illegal to dismiss the son of a bondwoman. We should remember that Ishmael was Abraham's only son for 14 years. Abraham's grief of Genesis 21:11 is quite understandable!

So God speaks words of reassurance and direction to Abraham. God's first pronouncement is that Sarah is right, *for in Isaac shall thy seed be called.* Isaac is indeed the son of the covenant. This fact contradicts the Islamic belief today that the covenant of promise goes through Ishmael.

Genesis 16:1 tells us that Hagar is an Egyptian. If she was given to Abraham (as Abram) by

Pharaoh in Genesis 12:14, it means she has been uprooted once already from familiar surroundings since Abraham is no longer in Egypt. Hagar tried to leave previously, of her own volition, because Sarah made her life miserable (Genesis 16). This time, however, Hagar is being expelled.

*What Do You Think?*

What can your church do to address the issue of dysfunctional families? What will be your part in this?

*Talking Points for Your Discussion*

- Prevention (premarital counseling, etc.)
- Intervention (family systems counseling, etc.)
- Other

**13. And also of the son of the bondwoman will I make a nation, because he is thy seed.**

Abraham's fears about what will happen to Ishmael are relieved: because Ishmael is a son of Abraham, the descendants of Ishmael will become a nation. Ishmael is a primary ancestor of many Arab peoples today (compare Genesis 25:12-18; 1 Chronicles 1:29).

### B. Dismissal (v. 14)

**14. And Abraham rose up early in the morning, and took bread, and a bottle of water, and gave it unto Hagar, putting it on her shoulder, and the child, and sent her away: and she departed, and wandered in the wilderness of Beersheba.**

Abraham obeys God's instructions without delay. Hagar and Ishmael are supplied with the basic necessities to begin their journey. The skin-bottle for the water is the normal container for liquids. We can only wonder if Hagar also receives gold or silver as part of her means to sustain herself.

The youthfulness of Ishmael is shown by the word *child.* Even so, he is at least 16 years old, as previously noted. Hagar's departure toward *the wilderness of Beersheba* indicates a move in a southeasterly direction.

### *The Danger of Impatience*

Troubled, dysfunctional families are far too common these days. The evidence of such trouble is often seen when a spouse—usually the wife—is found to be suffering from abuse. The abuser may use physical violence or the threat of it to exert control. The threats are themselves psychologically abusive.

The relationships within Abraham's family were troubled. We see abuse on the part of Sarah in Genesis 16:6 against Hagar. After Sarah bore Isaac, the child of God's promise, the stress between the two women reached a boiling point—again. Sarah demanded that Abraham "cast out" Hagar and Ishmael (21:10).

No doubt, Abraham thought he was doing the right thing (or, at least, the best thing in the circumstances) in sending the two away in order to restore peace in the home. Today this might be considered domestic abuse or, at least, "failure to support." But God was there to provide and protect when Abraham was not. We keep in mind that all this anguish could have been avoided had not Abraham and Sarah decided in their impatience to "help" God's plan by deciding to conceive a child by Hagar. Do you ever try to move faster than God wants you to? —C. R. B.

*What Do You Think?*

What are the limits of "tolerance," if any? Why?

*Talking Points for Your Discussion*

- Within families (Judges 11:1, 2; Acts 16:1)
- Within the church (John 1:14, 17; Romans 14; 1 Corinthians 5:11; 6:7, 8)
- In relationships with unbelievers (1 Corinthians 5:9, 10; 15:33)
- Other

### C. Assurance (vv. 17, 18)

**17. And God heard the voice of the lad; and the angel of God called to Hagar out of heaven, and said unto her, What aileth thee, Hagar? fear not; for God hath heard the voice of the lad where he is.**

Verses 15, 16 (not in today's text) indicate that the skin-bottle is soon empty. We do not know how much water has been supplied by Abraham or if Hagar has been able to refill the bottle to this point. In any case, the heat of the desert creates a great need for water, and it runs out.

Hagar (v. 16) and Ishmael are vocal in their distress. God responds because of *the voice of the lad,* but He directs his message to Hagar.

**18. Arise, lift up the lad, and hold him in thine hand; for I will make him a great nation.**

Hagar is not in the immediate presence of her son at this point; he is "a good way off, as it were a bowshot" (v. 16) when the angel of God speaks. The instruction to *hold him in thine hand* carries more than the idea of "physical holding"; Hagar is to be a guiding, steadying influence on her son. The angel of the Lord previously had told Hagar some things about the future of Ishmael when she ran away (see Genesis 16:11, 12). Now the promise is expanded: *I will make him a great nation.*

### D. Development (vv. 19-21)

**19. And God opened her eyes, and she saw a well of water; and she went, and filled the bottle with water, and gave the lad drink.**

God providentially supplies water. The presence of a well in this episode bears a similarity to the earlier occasion when Hagar fled from Sarah (Genesis 16:7). At that time, the angel of the Lord came to Hagar at a well (or "fountain," as it is called in 16:7), and it was given a name as a reminder of the event (16:14).

**20. And God was with the lad; and he grew, and dwelt in the wilderness, and became an archer.**

Two things combine to enable the hardy mother and son to survive in this rugged area. First is the fact that God is *with the lad.* Can any affirmation be better than that? Second, Ishmael develops his skill as an archer; this helps son and mother have an adequate food supply.

**21. And he dwelt in the wilderness of Paran: and his mother took him a wife out of the land of Egypt.**

The new home of Hagar and Ishmael *in the wilderness of Paran* means that the two have moved farther south. The region of Paran is in the Sinai Peninsula, which is just east of Egypt (compare Numbers 10:12). Ishmael needs a wife in order for him to become a great nation, so in a culture of arranged marriages, his mother turns to her native Egypt to meet that need (compare Genesis 24:1-4).

The rest of the story for Ishmael has several factors of interest. Genesis 25:7-9 states that Ishmael and Isaac are together again to bury Abraham when he dies at the age of 175. At that time Ishmael is age 89 and Isaac is 75. We can only wonder about the conversations and the farewells that took place!

Genesis 25:12-18 specifies that Ishmael has 12 sons and names them. The general regions where they live are listed. Ishmael will die at the age of 137, and the promises made to Abraham and Hagar indeed come to pass.

*What Do You Think?*

When did you see a plan fail, only to end up with a good (or better) outcome because it did? What did this experience teach you about God?

*Talking Points for Your Discussion*

- At work
- At church
- During a move
- Other

## II. Blessings for Isaac

(Genesis 26:2-5, 12, 13)

Isaac experiences many important events prior to the blessings listed in the next segment of today's printed text. His famous near-sacrifice is recorded in Genesis 22. The chapter that follows tells of the death of his mother at age 127, when Isaac is 37 years old and still single (compare 17:17 with 23:1). Abraham sends a trusted servant back to his relatives to secure a wife for Isaac (24:15), and that servant returns with Rebekah, who marries Isaac when he is 40 (25:20). She is a granddaughter of Nahor, Abraham's brother (and also a great-granddaughter of his other brother, Haran; see 11:29). Isaac at age 60 becomes the father of twins, Esau and Jacob (25:26).

A famine in Canaan then prompts Isaac to move his household elsewhere. The latter part of Genesis 26:1 seems to indicate that Isaac is already in Gerar. Isaac may intend this place to be no more than a stopover on the way to Egypt, but it ends up becoming a more permanent place of residence, as we shall see.

### A. Promises (vv. 2, 3)

**2. And the LORD appeared unto him, and said, Go not down into Egypt; dwell in the land which I shall tell thee of.**

Abraham had gone to Egypt in order to escape a famine over 100 years earlier. Egypt nearly always has good crops because of the annual surge of the Nile River. Isaac's descendants will go to Egypt in the days of Jacob also to escape a famine, but that is more than 100 years in the future at this point. From the time that Abram enters Canaan at age 75 (Genesis 12:4), there is a total of 215 years until grandson Jacob and the others go to Egypt (46:1-27). The Lord will command Jacob to do so at that time (46:3), but for now the Lord commands the opposite for Isaac, Jacob's father.

**3. Sojourn in this land, and I will be with thee, and will bless thee; for unto thee, and unto thy seed, I will give all these countries, and I will perform the oath which I sware unto Abraham thy father.**

Isaac needs to stay put. As Isaac does so, the Lord intends to bless him and *perform the oath* given to Abraham on more than one occasion.

This is the first of only two times that God provides a special message for Isaac (the other one is in Genesis 26:24). In addition, the Lord reveals to Rebekah, Isaac's wife, that she will have twins (25:23). This limited communication does not diminish Isaac's role as one of the great patriarchs. He is a man of faith, and this is affirmed in Hebrews 11:20. Isaac lives as God desires.

*What Do You Think?*

Under what circumstances would it be wise to advise someone to relocate rather than staying put? When would that be bad advice? Why?

*Talking Points for Your Discussion*

- Issues of God's call to mission work
- Issues of responsibility to family
- Issues of economic conditions
- Other

#### *TOWARD GREENER GRASS?*

"The grass is always greener on the other side of the fence" is a well-worn proverb. It's truth is said to be demonstrated by the fact that cattle and horses can be see standing at a fence row as they nibble at the grass growing just on the other side. If we look closely, however, we may see good reason for the livestock's behavior: the grass on their side of the fence may have already been eaten! So too we humans may have good reasons for seeking "greener grass."

Good things may come from such a desire. Think of the great explorers of centuries past. Whatever motivated them, we are the beneficiaries of their efforts. But bad things can also come from a desire to reach "greener grass" if we are merely trying to sidestep or escape our problems.

For Isaac and his family, Egypt seemed like a better place to live than Gerar. The annual flooding of the Nile River meant famines were less frequent there. Egypt's civilization seems to have been more advanced than other's. But God told Isaac not to go. There is a time to move on and a time to stay put; this is a matter for prayer. Our greatest personal growth may come in working through today's obstacles rather than bailing out.

—C. R. B.

### B. Posterity (vv. 4, 5)

**4. And I will make thy seed to multiply as the stars of heaven, and will give unto thy seed all these countries; and in thy seed shall all the nations of the earth be blessed.**

The comparison with *the stars of heaven* is similar to what was stated to Abram (before being renamed Abraham) in Genesis 15:5 (see lesson 6). The statement to Abram was given as much as 20 years before Isaac was born. Isaac surely has heard about it second hand, but it is good for him to hear it personally.

A second part of this blessing is also similar to what was promised to Abram—that those who descend from Isaac will receive territories of the various people-groups that inhabit the land of Canaan. See comments on Genesis 15:19-21 in lesson 6.

The most important part of this revelation is that through Isaac's *seed shall all the nations of the earth be blessed.* This phrase is reminiscent of the promise given to Abram in Genesis 12:3, just before he left Haran to begin his sojourn to the land that God would show him.

**5. Because that Abraham obeyed my voice, and kept my charge, my commandments, my statutes, and my laws.**

The faith that pleases God is the obedient faith that Paul speaks of in Romans 1:5; 16:26. Such faith has been demonstrated by Abraham, and now Isaac hears the same challenge directly from God.

This verse is fascinating because it hints that there are different types of obligations for the patriarchs. We would like to know more about God's *commandments, statutes,* and *laws* at this point in history, but God has chosen not to make further explanations part of the divine record. (This is over 500 years before Moses gives the law to Israel at Sinai.) We can only wonder about things such as the sacrificing of animals by Abel (Genesis 4:4), Noah (8:20), and Abraham (22:7).

*What Do You Think?*

What personal stories can you tell of someone's faithfulness producing benefits for a future generation?

*Talking Points for Your Discussion*

- Regarding a minister
- Regarding a teacher
- Regarding an ancestor
- Other

### C. Prosperity (vv. 12, 13)

**12. Then Isaac sowed in that land, and received in the same year an hundredfold: and the Lord blessed him.**

*That land* refers to the area around Gerar (Genesis 26:6). Verses 7-11 (not in today's text) give the account of Isaac's imitating his father with a falsehood in the same area (compare 20:1-13). After being rebuked by the local king, Isaac remains in the area and becomes very successful. The primary reason is the blessing of the Lord.

**13. And the man waxed great, and went forward, and grew until he became very great.**

The blessings from God continue! Isaac has grain for his own use, and he can sell any surplus. The verses that follow show that his wealth includes herds, flocks, and servants. Truly Isaac is blessed both spiritually and materially. This will cause problems with neighbors, but those pagans eventually come to see that Isaac is "blessed of the Lord" (Genesis 26:29).

## Conclusion

### A. It's Not a License!

It is good to be reminded of the promises and blessings for Ishmael and Isaac, for we know that neither was perfect in the sight of the Lord. Little is known about Ishmael, except that as a teenager he mocked his little brother. God still made promises to him. Isaac, for his part, seems to have been a very godly person. His falsehood to the people of Gerar is a blemish on his record, but God still blessed him.

It is also good to know that God loves sinners and blesses them (us). But the fact that God blessed others after they sinned is not to be used as a license to justify sin. God forgives, but genuine repentance comes first.

### B. Prayer

Thank You, Almighty God, for blessing those who helped bring the Messiah into the world. May I do my part in sharing the good news about Jesus so that others may be blessed. In His name, amen.

### C. Thought to Remember

When blessed, remember the source.

Visual for Lesson 8. *Start a discussion by pointing to this visual as you ask, "Under what circumstances is it most important to do this? Why?"*

# Involvement Learning

*Some of the activities below are also found in the helpful student book,* Adult Bible Class.
*Don't forget to download the free reproducible page from www.standardlesson.com to enhance your lesson!*

## Into the Lesson

*Option 1:* Distribute copies of the "God Bless You!" activity from the reproducible page, which you can download. Have learners work individually on this brief exercise to introduce the concept of *blessing.*

*Option 2:* Prepare flash cards for the following words related to mental states and emotions: *confusion, discontentment, contempt, despair, hope, jealousy, joy, kindness, resolution, satisfaction, sorrow.* Before class, ask one of your more "expressive" students to be prepared to stand before the class and demonstrate the emotions as you reveal cards (one by one) that only he or she can see. Ask the class to guess each emotion being dramatized, then show the card. Comment: "A range of human emotions fill the first part of our text today. Let's see if we can sort things out."

## Into the Word

Distribute large flash cards as described in Option 2 above (whether or not you chose to do that option) to various learners. Say, "As we listen to Genesis 21:8-21, hold up your card if you think the verse being read reflects the emotion on your card."

Have a good oral reader stand before the group to read Genesis 21:8-21 (which includes verses not in the printed text). Ask your reader to pause after reading each verse to allow time for learners to raise their cards. Class members may offer a variety of responses; encourage free discussion. You may wish to make your own list before class for comparison.

Next, distribute handouts that list the enumerated principles below. Say, "As we work our way through Genesis 26:2-5, 12, 13, think of how these statements *are* or *are not* apparent in God's dealings with Isaac. Jot notes on your handout." Read the text slowly, stopping after each verse to allow time for learners to make the connections.

1. When God says, "Stop!" then one must stop. 2. With God, a promise to the father is a promise to the son. 3. One of the greatest promises is that many will be blessed by the faithful obedience of the one. 4. Physical blessings may be considered spiritual blessings if recognized as coming from God. 5. Wealth is a blessing if one is aware that it comes from God's grace. 6. Heading away from the place of God's promise is heading in the wrong direction. 7. Faith passed from one generation to the next is an indication the older generation is doing something right.

*Option:* If you chose Option 1 under Into the Lesson, use discoveries to compare and contrast with the blessings of Ishmael and Isaac as you work through the two sections of today's text.

## Into Life

*Option 1:* Explore your learners' understanding of Islam's view of Isaac and Ishmael by asking, "What do Muslims believe about the two sons of Abraham discussed in today's lesson?" Do your own research in advance so you can correct misperceptions. At a minimum, you should note that Muslims believe they have inherited Ishmael's legacy, thus their claim that they too are "children of Abraham." Ask, "What are some strategies for presenting Jesus as the Son of God to Muslims?"

To challenge your learners to grow in this area, distribute copies of the "Witnessing to the Descendants of Ishmael" activity from the reproducible page as take-home work.

*Option 2:* Have learners pair off and discuss this question: "What is the most difficult decision regarding a personal relationship you have ever had to make?" After a few minutes, ask for volunteers to reveal in general terms (no names mentioned) what was discussed. (Caution: this intensely personal question may bring back painful memories that are best left undisturbed.) Ask, "How do we grow in Christ through such times of pain?

# The Blessing Passes to Jacob

**Devotional Reading:** John 4:1-15
**Background Scripture:** Genesis 27, 28; 32:22-30; 35:9-15

## Genesis 28:1a, 10-22

**1a And Isaac called Jacob, and blessed him.**

. . . . . . . . . . . . . . . . . . . . . . . . . .

**10 And Jacob went out from Beersheba, and went toward Haran.**

**11 And he lighted upon a certain place, and tarried there all night, because the sun was set; and he took of the stones of that place, and put them for his pillows, and lay down in that place to sleep.**

**12 And he dreamed, and behold a ladder set up on the earth, and the top of it reached to heaven: and behold the angels of God ascending and descending on it.**

**13 And, behold, the LORD stood above it, and said, I am the LORD God of Abraham thy father, and the God of Isaac: the land whereon thou liest, to thee will I give it, and to thy seed;**

**14 And thy seed shall be as the dust of the earth, and thou shalt spread abroad to the west, and to the east, and to the north, and to the south: and in thee and in thy seed shall all the families of the earth be blessed.**

**15 And, behold, I am with thee, and will keep thee in all places whither thou goest, and will bring thee again into this land; for I will not leave thee, until I have done that which I have spoken to thee of.**

**16 And Jacob awaked out of his sleep, and he said, Surely the LORD is in this place; and I knew it not.**

**17 And he was afraid, and said, How dreadful is this place! this is none other but the house of God, and this is the gate of heaven.**

**18 And Jacob rose up early in the morning, and took the stone that he had put for his pillows, and set it up for a pillar, and poured oil upon the top of it.**

**19 And he called the name of that place Bethel: but the name of that city was called Luz at the first.**

**20 And Jacob vowed a vow, saying, If God will be with me, and will keep me in this way that I go, and will give me bread to eat, and raiment to put on,**

**21 So that I come again to my father's house in peace; then shall the LORD be my God:**

**22 And this stone, which I have set for a pillar, shall be God's house: and of all that thou shalt give me I will surely give the tenth unto thee.**

## Key Verse

*Behold, I am with thee, and will keep thee in all places whither thou goest, and will bring thee again into this land; for I will not leave thee, until I have done that which I have spoken to thee of.* —**Genesis 28:15**

# First Things

## Unit 2: First Nation

Lessons 6–9

## Lesson Aims

After participating in this lesson, each student will be able to:

1. Summarize the context and content of Jacob's dream at Bethel and his reaction to it.
2. Compare and contrast the "awakening" of someone to God's presence today with Jacob's sudden awareness of God's presence.
3. Suggest one or two ways to demonstrate actively his or her awareness of God's presence.

## Lesson Outline

Introduction
- A. If? Because? Regardless?
- B. Lesson Background

I. Isaac Blesses (Genesis 28:1a)

II. Jacob Dreams (Genesis 28:10-15)
- A. Sleep Achieved (vv. 10, 11)
- B. Imagery Perceived (vv. 12, 13a)
- C. Promise Received (vv. 13b-15)
  - *Jacob's Dream as Ours*

III. Jacob Reacts (Genesis 28:16-22)
- A. Great Fear (vv. 16, 17)
  - *"I Didn't Know . . ."*
- B. Stone Memorial (v. 18)
- C. New Name (v. 19)
- D. Special Vow (vv. 20-22)

Conclusion
- A. What Next?
- B. Prayer
- C. Thought to Remember

## Introduction

### A. If? Because? Regardless?

It is interesting to classify levels of faith by the three words above. Examples of the three levels abound.

*The "if" level.* This level is characterized by an attitude of "If (and only if) God will do *this*, then I will do *that*." Some people bargain with God to coax Him to do what they want. In other words, their obedience to God is conditional. A statement by Jacob that is part of today's lesson may seem, at first glance, to demonstrate this level. We will evaluate this in our discussion of Genesis 28:20, 21.

*The "because" level.* We may perceive this level of faith in passages such as Exodus 18:11; Judges 17:13; 1 Kings 17:24; and 2 Kings 5:15. Particularly interesting is Job 1:9-11. There Satan claims that Job fears God *because* God has blessed him so much; but if God were to remove the blessings, then Job would curse God. Job proved that his faith was not what Satan thought. Instead, Job's faith was at the next level.

*The "regardless" level.* Job 13:15 speaks to this level of faith. This level also is demonstrated by Daniel's three friends who refused to bow to an idol near Babylon. The three men stated that God was able to deliver them; but even if God chose not to deliver them, they still would not bow to the image (Daniel 3:16-18).

These three levels of faith and today's lesson text invite each of us to consider this question: Which level of faith describes my own?

### B. Lesson Background

The final segment of last week's lesson saw Isaac becoming ever more prosperous (Genesis 26:13). That prosperity, however, brought negative consequences in the forms of jealousy, sabotage, and expulsion (vv. 14-16). As a result, Isaac ended up moving to the southeast, toward Beersheba (v. 23), a place where his father, Abraham, had lived.

It was at Beersheba that the elderly Isaac decided that it was time for him to give the formal patriarchal blessing to his older son, Esau (Genesis 27:4). This was in spite of the fact that God had told Rebekah that the older would serve the younger

(25:23). Isaac may have reasoned that Esau should have the blessing because Esau already had wives (26:34) whereas Jacob was still a bachelor.

Things did not go as Isaac had planned because Rebekah schemed for Jacob to receive the blessing instead (Genesis 27:5-29). This was accomplished, but then Esau threatened to kill his brother (27:41). Rebekah heard about the threat, and she developed a plan to put her favored son 550 miles away: she appealed to Isaac that Jacob should return to her relatives in order to secure a proper wife (26:34, 35; 27:46). Our text for today picks up with Isaac's reaction to this plan.

## I. Isaac Blesses

(Genesis 28:1a)

**1a. And Isaac called Jacob, and blessed him.**

Isaac has already blessed Jacob once (Genesis 27:27-29); that blessing was for prosperity and dominance. The blessing we see here is for Jacob to find a proper wife. Rebekah has expressed to Isaac, her husband, her displeasure with Esau's wives. They are "daughters of Heth" (27:46); Heth is the ancestor of the Hittites (10:15; 23:10; 26:34).

Genesis 28:1b-5 (not in today's text) describes Isaac's instructions for Jacob to secure a wife in far away Padanaram. Verses 6-9 reveal Esau's sensitivity about his parents' feelings toward his wives; in an attempt to compensate, he marries a first cousin, a daughter of Ishmael.

*What Do You Think?*

When was a time you were blessed by respecting someone else's wishes?

*Talking Points for Your Discussion*

- Concerning a parent
- Concerning a friend
- Concerning your church's leadership
- Other

## II. Jacob Dreams

(Genesis 28:10-15)

### A. Sleep Achieved (vv. 10, 11)

**10. And Jacob went out from Beersheba, and went toward Haran.**

As Jacob departs, he may wonder if he will ever see his parents again. This concern seems to enter into the vow that he makes later (v. 21, below). Jacob does see his father again (Genesis 35:27-29). But as far as can be determined, Jacob does not see his mother again; the last time Rebekah is understood to be living is here in chapter 28.

Genesis 26:34 states that Esau is 40 years old when he marries two Hittite women. Jacob's age when he leaves his parents to find a wife is not stated. Circumstantial data based on subsequent events are used by some scholars to suggest that he is 77 years old when he leaves his parents, with an alternative view that he is 57. Jacob's destination is Haran, the place where grandfather Abraham was living before he left for Canaan (Genesis 11:31).

**11. And he lighted upon a certain place, and tarried there all night, because the sun was set; and he took of the stones of that place, and put them for his pillows, and lay down in that place to sleep.**

Travel at night is difficult and unwise in an era before streetlights. Therefore, it is time to stop when the sun sets. The *certain place* where Jacob stops is named Luz, which Jacob will rename Bethel per verse 19, below. This is almost 60 miles from Jacob's starting point in Beersheba, so this is probably his second or third night on the road, depending on his speed of travel.

Two meals per day are customary, and perhaps Jacob has the second of these before bedding down for the night. His meal may be something his mother prepared for him, which is possible at this stage of the journey. But Jacob will have to live off the land as the journey progresses (v. 20).

We may wonder how Jacob intends to get much sleep if he is using stones for pillows! But this will be no ordinary night of sleep in any case.

### B. Imagery Perceived (vv. 12, 13a)

**12. And he dreamed, and behold a ladder set up on the earth, and the top of it reached to heaven: and behold the angels of God ascending and descending on it.**

Jacob's sleep this night involves dreaming, and this becomes a spiritual highlight. This is the first of several times that the Lord communicates directly with Jacob, and it is the second time that dreams are used by God to give a message to someone. (The first time is in Genesis 20:3.) Dreams become very important in the remainder of Genesis; they involve Jacob and Laban plus four other people in the days of Joseph.

As Jacob looks he sees *the angels of God ascending and descending* on some kind of ladder. An Internet search will reveal numerous artistic efforts to depict this. Some students propose that this ladder is something like the ancient ziggurats, which have sets of stairs to connect different levels. Archaeologists have discovered that the steps of the ziggurats were for gods to come down from Heaven; the purpose of the tower at Babel was to reach to the heavens (see lesson 5).

Jacob's dream is different: it has angels moving in both directions between Heaven and earth. Jesus used phrases from this verse in his discussion with Nathanael (see John 1:51).

**13a. And, behold, the LORD stood above it.**

Jacob is probably aware of the pagan concepts mentioned above. If he is, then he realizes that what he sees in his dream is different from paganism in an important way: the Lord is standing above the ladder, and there is no movement on His part to come to earth.

*What Do You Think?*

What's the difference between dreams from God and "regular" dreams? How do those differences serve as a caution about claiming "God told me . . ." because of a dream?

*Talking Points for Your Discussion*

- The content of the dream
- The uniqueness of the dream
- The circumstances of the dream
- Jeremiah 23:25-32
- Revelation 22:18, 19
- Other

### C. Promise Received (vv. 13b-15)

**13b. And said, I am the LORD God of Abraham thy father, and the God of Isaac: the land whereon thou liest, to thee will I give it, and to thy seed.**

Jacob secured his brother's birthright by bargaining for it, and he received his father's patriarchal blessing by deception. But Jacob is now given a promise that is immensely more important than either of those two: the announcement that the blessings promised through Abraham and Isaac are to continue through him. This is the most important part of the dream. Jacob also learns that his mission will be successful; the fact that the land will be given to Jacob's seed means that he will have a wife and at least one child.

The promise about possessing the land was first given to Abraham (Genesis 12:6, 7), then repeated after he returned from Egypt (15:18-21; lesson 6). The land-promise to Abraham was to that man's "seed," while the restatement here is to both Jacob's seed and to Jacob himself.

We may wonder why God applies the word *father* to Abraham instead of Isaac since Abraham was actually Jacob's grandfather. The word *father* is used in the Bible also to describe "ancestors"; likewise, the word *son* is used to describe "successors." Abraham was Jacob's "father" in a special way.

**14. And thy seed shall be as the dust of the earth, and thou shalt spread abroad to the west, and to the east, and to the north, and to the south: and in thee and in thy seed shall all the families of the earth be blessed.**

The Lord's message continues, and a phrase is used that Jacob probably has heard before—that the posterity of this family *shall be as the dust of the earth.* This phrase was used when Abraham separated from Lot and as Abraham was promised all the land he could see (Genesis 13:14-18). Jacob may have heard about this from his grandfather personally, for Jacob was 15 when Abraham died (computed from 21:5; 25:7, 20, 26).

The part of the message about the blessing to come on *all the families of the earth* was first stated in Genesis 12:3, when Abraham was leaving Haran (the place Jacob is now headed). This has been God's larger plan all along. It is not a new element.

**15. And, behold, I am with thee, and will keep thee in all places whither thou goest, and will bring thee again into this land; for I will not leave thee, until I have done that which I have spoken to thee of.**

The story of the assurance that Jacob received of the Lord's presence for the journey will be passed along to the Israelites by Moses just before that man's death hundreds of years later (Deuteronomy 31:6). However, the message of assurance in the verse before us is not merely for Jacob himself. God has bigger plans in mind, as seen in the last phrase of Genesis 28:14, above. The Lord will bring to pass all the things that He has declared. Jacob knows that his mission will be successful, and he learns that he will be able to return to Canaan.

### *Jacob's Dream as Ours*

We use the word *dream* in various ways. Very often this word has a sense of "unreality" attached to it. All of us have told stories of the weird things we dream of while asleep. Those as well as most of our daydreams are nothing more than fantasies (compare Psalm 73:20; Isaiah 29:8).

Dream-fantasies make for good songwriting. "I Dream of Jeannie with the Light Brown Hair" is the first line of a song of similar name published in 1854. Moving into the twentieth century, we have songs such as "Dream a Little Dream of Me." There is even a list of "25 Hit Songs Named After Dreams" on the Internet!

The message God gave to Jacob was not a fantasy composed to entertain people at a social gathering. God's dream-message to Jacob renewed the promise that God would be with His people to be a blessing to the nations. This dream-message is important to us as well; we help bring it ever closer to fulfillment as we carry out the Great Commission (Matthew 28:19, 20). —C. R. B.

## HOW TO SAY IT

| | |
|---|---|
| Babel | *Bay*-bul. |
| Babylon | *Bab*-uh-lun. |
| Beersheba | Beer-*she*-buh. |
| Bethel | *Beth*-ul. |
| Canaan | *Kay*-nun. |
| Esau | *Ee*-saw. |
| Haran | *Hair*-un. |
| Hittite | *Hit*-ites or *Hit*-tite. |
| Ishmael | *Ish*-may-el. |
| Nathanael | Nuh-*than*-yull (*th* as in *thin*). |
| patriarchal | pay-tree-*are*-kul. |
| Rebekah | Reh-*bek*-uh. |
| ziggurats | *zig*-oo-rats. |

## III. Jacob Reacts

(Genesis 28:16-22)

### A. Great Fear (vv. 16, 17)

**16, 17. And Jacob awaked out of his sleep, and he said, Surely the Lord is in this place; and I knew it not. And he was afraid, and said, How dreadful is this place! this is none other but the house of God, and this is the gate of heaven.**

As Jacob awakes, he quickly reacts to what he has experienced. The statement *the Lord is in this place* may seem curious at first. Doesn't Jacob know that God is everywhere? About 1,000 years later, David will affirm in Psalm 139:7-12 that he cannot escape from God, for God is indeed everywhere. Jacob may not realize that fact at this point in his life, or he simply may be reacting from terror since the word *dreadful* conveys the idea of "fear."

The positions of the standing Lord and the moving angels draw Jacob's conclusion that *this is the gate of heaven.* We think of a gate as something that allows or blocks access to something else. Therefore Jacob's present location seems to be a special piece of geography. The phrase *the house of God* will be considered when we get to verse 19.

*What Do You Think?*

In what places or situations have you sensed God's presence where you otherwise felt isolated? Why was that?

*Talking Points for Your Discussion*

- During a military deployment
- During a personal crisis
- While convalescing
- During a family conflict
- Other

### *"I Didn't Know . . ."*

Douglas "Wrong Way" Corrigan (1907–1995) became famous for his transatlantic flight of 1938. Taking off from Brooklyn, New York, he flew nonstop to Ireland although his flight plan

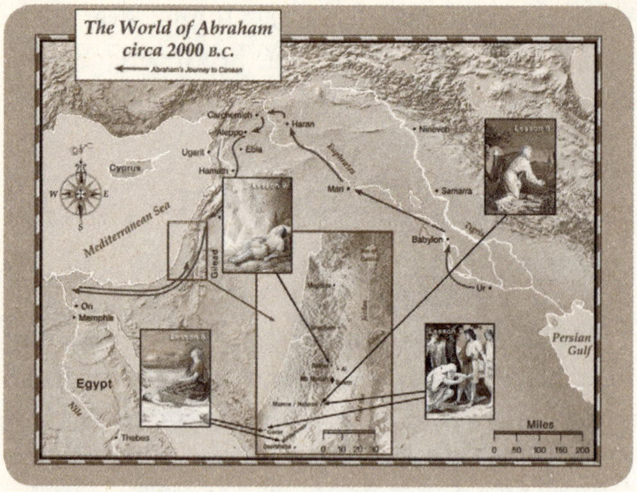


Visual for Lessons 6 & 9. *Wrap up this unit of lessons by summarizing the faith that was evident as you point to the four smallest insets in sequence.*

called for him to fly to Long Beach, California. He claimed to have discovered he was going the wrong way about 26 hours into the 28-hour flight, citing navigational error due to heavy cloud cover. Although the evidence pointed to an intentional "error," Corrigan stuck to his story of not knowing he was going the wrong direction. Some claims of "I didn't know" are hard to swallow!

Jacob's claim, "Surely the Lord is in this place; and I knew it not" is more believable. He did not claim to have ended up in Bethel by navigational error, and he was not out to set up a profitable tourist attraction. With the revelation of the New Testament, we must acknowledge that "surely the Lord is in this place" wherever we go; the "and I knew it not" part of Jacob's statement is not available to us. May we not live in self-imposed ignorance to the evidence of God's presence in our lives! —C. R. B.

### B. Stone Memorial (v. 18)

**18. And Jacob rose up early in the morning, and took the stone that he had put for his pillows, and set it up for a pillar, and poured oil upon the top of it.**

A custom then as now is to erect memorials to commemorate events, battles, etc. Large stone pillars or slabs of stone are used to help both present and future generations remember what happened in a place. What Jacob is doing here fits this pattern (see also Genesis 31:45-53; 35:1-15, 20).

Some suggest that this procedure is in conflict with what Moses stresses in Deuteronomy 16:22—that the people of Israel are not to set up sacred images or stones, for the Lord hates them. The resolution of this supposed conflict is simple. If an erected stone is to involve the worship of other gods, then the Lord's statement applies. A stone memorial is entirely different, however (compare Exodus 24:4; Joshua 4:1-9).

The next act involving Jacob's memorial stone is to dedicate or consecrate it. This is done by pouring oil on the top of the stone. Oil is connected with consecration or anointing in many places in the Old Testament; the one we see here is the first.

### C. New Name (v. 19)

**19. And he called the name of that place Bethel: but the name of that city was called Luz at the first.**

Jacob does two more things before resuming his journey. In verse 17 he declared that the place where he has just slept is "the house of God"; now Jacob determines to use this expression as the name for this location, which is about 11 miles north of Jerusalem. The syllable *beth* means "house of" in Hebrew, and *el* is a shortened word for "God." Therefore *Bethel* means "house of God." Since *Bethel . . . was called Luz at the first,* we may wonder why Moses, who wrote this account, states that Abram "removed from [Haran] unto a mountain on the east of Bethel, and pitched his tent, having Bethel on the west" (Genesis 12:8). Undoubtedly, Moses did this for the sake of clarity.

Bethel will play an important part in the history of Israel. The town becomes a center of idol worship after the nation splits apart in about 930 BC (1 Kings 12:25-33), but Bethel's idolatrous altar will be destroyed by a godly king hundreds of years after that (2 Kings 23:15). Archaeologists have not been able to determine with certainty the location of Bethel.

### D. Special Vow (vv. 20-22)

**20. And Jacob vowed a vow, saying, If God will be with me, and will keep me in this way that I go, and will give me bread to eat, and raiment to put on.**

Jacob's final decision involves something that is not recorded in the Bible until now: the making of a vow to God. Vows made to deities often include conditions: "only if the deity will do *this* will I then do *that.*" While many people attempt to negotiate terms with God, that does not seem to be the case for Jacob. For Jacob, the context of his situation is one of appreciation, not the "if" level of faith that was cited in the lesson Introduction. Reverence is a factor motivating him to want to do something for the God of Abraham and Isaac, who has now affirmed that the special promises will continue through Jacob.

*What Do You Think?*

Are vows to God appropriate in the New Testament era? Why, or why not?

*Talking Points for Your Discussion*

- Matthew 5:33-37; 23:16-22
- Acts 18:18; 21:18-26
- Hebrews 6:16
- James 5:12

**21, 22. So that I come again to my father's house in peace; then shall the LORD be my God: and this stone, which I have set for a pillar, shall be God's house: and of all that thou shalt give me I will surely give the tenth unto thee.**

Jacob's financial holdings are negligible as he makes this vow. He has only what is with him. If Jacob is ever able to return to his *father's house,* then Jacob will do his best to fulfill his sincere desires to make this place *God's house* and to *give the tenth* of all he has. This verse is usually viewed from the perspective of what Jacob accumulates while he is away (see Genesis 30:43), but he does not know of any future wealth at this point.

The tithe or tenth in the ancient world is usually a tax given to a ruler. The context shows that Jacob's desire to give a tenth to God is in appreciation for God's working through him to accomplish God's purposes. Jacob reasons that he first has to return *(come again to my father's house in peace)* in order to receive his inheritance. The birthright portion is ordinarily twice what anyone else receives (compare Deuteronomy 21:17), and Jacob is in possession of that birthright.

Admittedly, Jacob has his faults; one such fault will present itself years later when Jacob rebukes his favorite son for having a dream (Genesis 37:10)! But one emphasis here is that Jacob sincerely wants to pass something back to God because of what God promises him. God will remind Jacob of his vow years later (31:13, 38).

*What Do You Think?*

When did a sense of God's presence make a difference in how you reacted to a difficult time in your life? How did things turn out?

*Talking Points for Your Discussion*

- During an "alone time" of intense soul-searching
- During a church conflict
- During a family conflict
- Other

## Conclusion

### A. What Next?

We would like to know more about Jacob's mind-set as he left Beersheba. His brother intended to kill him, and he had to leave for his own safety. His scheming had not produced what he had wanted, so he ended up on the road, alone.

In some cases, it is a good thing to have everything go wrong and to end up at the bottom. From this position it is easier to look up to God and to trust in Him. Even then, some people seem to experience more than their "share" of poverty and/or persecution. To be a Christian in some cultures is to be oppressed continually.

Regardless of the situations of life, the real question is *What responses to my situation will be pleasing to God?* Jacob made good choices at Bethel. Each person has choices to make in "the house of God." What will yours be?

### B. Prayer

Father, I want to honor You in all circumstances. Please grant me the wisdom to make right choices throughout this day. In Jesus' name, amen.

### C. Thought to Remember

Christians are always in Bethel,
the house of God.

# Involvement Learning

*Some of the activities below are also found in the helpful student book,* Adult Bible Class.
*Don't forget to download the free reproducible page from www.standardlesson.com to enhance your lesson!*

## Into the Lesson

Hold up a bed pillow as class begins. Ask, "Does anyone need some sleep?" After some reactions, say, "Well, Jacob certainly needed some sleep." Then pull out a large, rounded rock and say, "Here's what Jacob found to rest his head on. Anyone want to try it? You might need to wrap your coat around it a few times!"

Next, display the words *If / Because / Regardless* vertically on the board, with *If* at the top. Put the word *Faith* on a strip of poster board, and hold this strip alongside each of the other three words in sequence as you lead the class in saying in unison the two-word phrases that result: *"if" faith / "because" faith / "regardless" faith.* Ask, "What are the differences among these types or levels of faith?" Use the lesson Introduction to clarify learners' responses. Say, "Let's see how today's text can help move us to the *regardless* level.

## Into the Word

Display the stub of an airplane boarding pass (actual or created), a compass, a flashlight, a stone, a toy ladder, an angel figurine, some seeds, a globe, a bottle of olive oil, a contract, and a church offering envelope. Draw attention to each item briefly in the order given; then return each to a table in front of the group. Say, "See if you can tell me how each of these relate to the story in today's text." Have the text read aloud.

Learners should note the following connections as the story unfolds: the ticket represents Jacob's journey; the compass represents Jacob's travel in a certain direction and the four directions of verse 14; the flashlight is for the nighttime scene; the stone represents Jacob's "pillow"; the ladder is for the conduit between earth and Heaven; the angel represents those Jacob sees ascending and descending; the seeds stand for Jacob's future family; the globe suggests that "all the families of the earth [will] be blessed"; the oil represents the dedication of the pillar; the contract illustrates God's promise and Jacob's vow; the envelope represents the tithe Jacob promises.

Bring the text into modern experience by asking this question: "In what ways can Jacob's experience be similar to the ways people today might sense God's special presence?" Learners may note that a sense of God's closeness may be sudden and unexpected and/or may occur when in a quiet, thoughtful state of mind.

Follow up by asking, "What aspects of Jacob's experience should we *not* expect to be repeated today? Why?" This may lead into a discussion of individuals who claim that "God told me" such and such. Be prepared to address the dangers of "them that prophesy out of their own hearts" because of "a vain vision" and "a lying divination" (Ezekiel 13:1, 2, 7). Discuss the infrequent nature of God-given dreams in the Bible.

## Into Life

*Option 1:* Give each learner a card with this incomplete statement: "God is here, and I know it because . . ." Say, "We all need to raise our awareness of the personal presence of God. This week, carry this card and jot notes when you sense God's nearness. As the week concludes, ask yourself this question: 'What similarities do I see in the occasions I have noted?'"

*Option 2:* Distribute copies of the "When and Where" activity from the reproducible page, which you can download. Ask learners to take a few minutes to complete it. Ask for volunteers to share thoughts with the class, but don't put anyone on the spot.

*Option 3:* The "Why and How" activity on the reproducible page can help reinforce the idea of giving more attention to the way God is at work in one's life. This can be a take-home exercise if you think learners will hesitate to share the personal responses.

# God Prepares for Deliverance

Devotional Reading: Exodus 4:10-16
Background Scripture: Exodus 1–4

## Exodus 3:7-17

**7 And the Lord said, I have surely seen the affliction of my people which are in Egypt, and have heard their cry by reason of their taskmasters; for I know their sorrows;**

**8 And I am come down to deliver them out of the hand of the Egyptians, and to bring them up out of that land unto a good land and a large, unto a land flowing with milk and honey; unto the place of the Canaanites, and the Hittites, and the Amorites, and the Perizzites, and the Hivites, and the Jebusites.**

**9 Now therefore, behold, the cry of the children of Israel is come unto me: and I have also seen the oppression wherewith the Egyptians oppress them.**

**10 Come now therefore, and I will send thee unto Pharaoh, that thou mayest bring forth my people the children of Israel out of Egypt.**

**11 And Moses said unto God, Who am I, that I should go unto Pharaoh, and that I should bring forth the children of Israel out of Egypt?**

**12 And he said, Certainly I will be with thee; and this shall be a token unto thee, that I have sent thee: When thou hast brought forth the people out of Egypt, ye shall serve God upon this mountain.**

**13 And Moses said unto God, Behold, when I come unto the children of Israel, and shall say unto them, The God of your fathers hath sent me unto you; and they shall say to me, What is his name? what shall I say unto them?**

**14 And God said unto Moses, I AM THAT I AM: and he said, Thus shalt thou say unto the children of Israel, I AM hath sent me unto you.**

**15 And God said moreover unto Moses, Thus shalt thou say unto the children of Israel, The Lord God of your fathers, the God of Abraham, the God of Isaac, and the God of Jacob, hath sent me unto you: this is my name for ever, and this is my memorial unto all generations.**

**16 Go, and gather the elders of Israel together, and say unto them, The Lord God of your fathers, the God of Abraham, of Isaac, and of Jacob, appeared unto me, saying, I have surely visited you, and seen that which is done to you in Egypt:**

**17 And I have said, I will bring you up out of the affliction of Egypt unto the land of the Canaanites, and the Hittites, and the Amorites, and the Perizzites, and the Hivites, and the Jebusites, unto a land flowing with milk and honey.**

## Key Verses

*The Lord God of your fathers, the God of Abraham, of Isaac, and of Jacob, appeared unto me, saying, I have surely visited you, and seen that which is done to you in Egypt: and I have said, I will bring you up out of the affliction of Egypt.* —**Exodus 3:16b, 17a**

# First Things

## Unit 3: First Freedom

Lessons 10–13

## Lesson Aims

After participating in this lesson, each student will be able to:

1. Summarize God's call to Moses and Moses' reaction to it.

2. Explain the meaning and significance of God's name.

3. Plan a specific way to be a voice for someone facing oppression today.

## Lesson Outline

Introduction

- A. Prince of Egypt
- B. Lesson Background

I. God Sees (Exodus 3:7-10)

- A. Awareness of Suffering (v. 7)
  - *The All-Seeing God*
- B. Declaration of Solution (vv. 8, 9)
- C. Commissioning of Moses (v. 10)

II. God Explains (Exodus 3:11-15)

- A. Doubt and Assurance (vv. 11, 12)
  - *Reluctant to Serve*
- B. Question and Answer (vv. 13-15)

III. God Sends (Exodus 3:16, 17)

- A. Elders Assembled (v. 16)
- B. Plan Announced (v. 17)

Conclusion

- A. Servant of God
- B. Prayer
- C. Thought to Remember

## Introduction

### A. Prince of Egypt

In 1998, DreamWorks Animation released the animated film *Prince of Egypt.* This popular movie retells the story of the deliverance of the Israelites from Egypt.

As is often the case with cinematic retellings, the producers take considerable liberty with the story. Although the Bible says nothing about Moses' life growing up as the adopted son of Pharaoh's daughter, the movie furnishes abundant details. In the movie, Moses is adopted not by Pharaoh's daughter, but by the queen. That makes Moses the stepson of Pharaoh and kid brother to Ramses, who is next in line to succeed his father as Pharaoh. Moses therefore ends up wielding considerable power as Royal Chief Architect under his brother, who is crown prince in charge of all of Pharaoh's temple building projects.

Moses is oblivious to his humble origins as the son of a Hebrew slave at first. But Miriam, his sister by birth, reveals the truth to him. Although he is reluctant to accept it, this truth is confirmed by a disturbing dream and a frank conversation with his stepparents.

DreamWorks Animation is not alone in filling the gaps in Moses' backstory. It is quite common for preachers, Sunday school teachers, and even Bible scholars to infer a great deal from the simple statement, "And the child grew, and she brought him unto Pharaoh's daughter, and he became her son" (Exodus 2:10). Who can blame them? Moses is a pivotal figure in both biblical and world history. Three of the major world religions (Christianity, Judaism, and Islam) claim Moses as a core prophet. Today we will look at what Scripture does have to say about the event that changed the course of Moses' life and world history.

### B. Lesson Background

In Genesis 15, God appeared to Abraham in a vision to reaffirm the promise to make a great nation of that man. God sealed His Word with a covenant ceremony (lesson 6). Though this was certainly good news to Abraham, a dark cloud hovered over this promise: God also revealed to

Abraham that his descendants would be enslaved in Egypt for 400 years (v. 13).

That is precisely what happened. Abraham's grandson Jacob was forced to relocate all of Abraham's descendants to Egypt in about 1877 BC to survive a famine (Genesis 45–50). Things went well at first. Through divine providence, Jacob's son Joseph had received Pharaoh's favor and was able to settle all of his extended family in the rich land of Goshen.

The Israelites multiplied as time passed, but the memory of Joseph's favor evaporated from the Egyptian establishment (Exodus 1:8). The Israelites came to be seen as a threat within their host country. So the Pharaohs followed the well-trod path of paranoid power-bearers: they intensified their grip and oppressed this minority (vv. 9-11).

Things seemed bleak for Abraham's descendants, but the birth of Moses changed everything. Because Pharaoh had issued a decree that all Israelite boys were to be killed at birth, Moses' mother placed him in the river in "an ark of bulrushes" (Exodus 2:3). Pharaoh's daughter soon discovered him and proceeded to ask Moses' mother to nurse the infant. The daughter then adopted Moses as her own (vv. 5-10).

The next we hear of Moses is when he killed an Egyptian for mistreating a Hebrew slave (Exodus 2:12). Unlike the animated film, however, Pharaoh exhibited no special affection for Moses and ordered him to be executed (v. 15). Moses fled and found a new home among the Midianites, who lived east of Egypt (vv. 11-22).

Then Moses found God—or God found Moses! While tending sheep, Moses saw a bush that burned without being consumed (Exodus 3:2, 3). Moses listened as God revealed His will to Moses, who was 80 years old at the time (7:7).

## I. God Sees

(Exodus 3:7-10)

### A. Awareness of Suffering (v. 7)

**7. And the Lord said, I have surely seen the affliction of my people which are in Egypt, and have heard their cry by reason of their taskmasters; for I know their sorrows.**

Our passage begins with God. In so doing, the verse before us establishes something that Christians have long claimed by faith: God sees and hears. The God of Israel, who later reveals himself as the God of Jesus, sees the plight and hears the cries of His people. He is neither blind nor deaf (contrast Psalms 115:4-7; 135:15-17).

After 400 years of exile, Abraham's descendants may have grown callous to claims about God's promise to make them a great nation. The fact that the reception Moses later receives from his own people runs both hot (Exodus 4:29-31) and cold (5:19-21; 6:9) testifies that time has taken its toll on their faith. The Lord is appearing to Moses at a time when the people fear for their lives. The new Pharaoh has not only increased their labor (1:8-14), but also is murdering their baby boys (1:15-22). The taskmasters have become ruthless in using the Hebrews as slaves to carry out backbreaking labor in the heat of the sun (1:11-14). In an environment like this, the last thing the Hebrews want is for someone to stir up trouble and provoke Pharaoh to make their lives even more miserable.

*What Do You Think?*

Do biblical examples of complaint and despair ever serve as models of how we should pray? Why, or why not?

*Talking Points for Your Discussion*

- Job 6:1-4
- Psalm 44:23-26
- Lamentations 3:44

### *The All-Seeing God*

George Orwell's dark novel *1984* presents the specter of government as an all-seeing Big Brother, capable of intruding into every aspect of people's lives. The fear of the ever-increasing ability of government to "watch us" has intensified over the six decades since the book's appearance. As one website claims, "If you think the government is watching your every move, that's crazy—but if you think the government is too good or too honest to try it, that's naïve."

Surveillance is not limited to the government, however. We all know that we are being watched by cameras on private property such as banks and shopping malls—any place where criminal activity is likely. And the proliferation of cellphone cameras in the hands of the masses means that *whatever* we do in public (and sometimes in private) has the potential of appearing online for everyone to see. Our cherished privacy is no more.

But there has never been such a thing as privacy from God's eyes! As God saw the suffering of the ancient Hebrews, so also He sees everything about our lives. Whether you find that fact to be comforting or frightening speaks volumes about your spiritual condition. —C. R. B.

### B. Declaration of Solution (vv. 8, 9)

**8. And I am come down to deliver them out of the hand of the Egyptians, and to bring them up out of that land unto a good land and a large, unto a land flowing with milk and honey; unto the place of the Canaanites, and the Hittites, and the Amorites, and the Perizzites, and the Hivites, and the Jebusites.**

God's response is not merely that of declaring His awareness. He is not the kind of god whom people imagine as knowing what is going on but choosing not to get involved. The true God acts! He steers world history toward its appointed end. Central to God's plans for world history is His desire to form Abraham's descendants into a people to bless all nations (Genesis 12:1-3).

That blessing requires the Hebrews to occupy a particular plot of land between the Mediterranean Sea and the Jordan River: the land of Canaan (or Palestine). This is the first of 20 passages in the Old Testament to refer to this land as *flowing with milk and honey.* This phrase conveys an image of a fertile land that is ideally suited for farming and animal husbandry. When compared with many other parts of the world today, Palestine may not seem all that fertile. But when compared with the lands around it in Moses' day, it stands out as prime real estate in what is called the Fertile Crescent.

The commentary on verse 17 below discusses the particular people groups listed in this verse (see also lesson 6).

**9. Now therefore, behold, the cry of the children of Israel is come unto me: and I have also seen the oppression wherewith the Egyptians oppress them.**

The all-knowing God is about to teach both His people and the Egyptians that He is no mere tribal or territorial deity. *The children of Israel* will eventually learn that their God is the God of all nations; the oppressive wickedness of Egypt draws God's attention just as much as the well-being of Israel does.

All this will be evident when God unleashes the 10 plagues on Egypt (Exodus 7–12). After that, God will continue His judgment because the Egyptians will have much to learn as the oppressors become the oppressed. What the Egyptians will not learn until much later is that God's people must be released so that God can use them to incorporate Egypt and all other nations into His saving purposes in Christ (Matthew 28:19; Galatians 3:8).

### C. Commissioning of Moses (v. 10)

**10. Come now therefore, and I will send thee unto Pharaoh, that thou mayest bring forth my people the children of Israel out of Egypt.**

Up to this point, Moses may be thrilled at what he is hearing. The focus so far has been on God's saving actions on Israel's behalf. Now, however, God is recruiting Moses to implement the plan!

Moses' assignment is far more dangerous than merely speaking to the Hebrews and organizing their departure. He must return to the capital city, where a warrant out for his arrest was once issued

## HOW TO SAY IT

| | |
|---|---|
| Amorites | *Am*-uh-rites. |
| Canaanites | *Kay*-nun-ites. |
| Girgashites | *Gur*-guh-shites. |
| Jebusites | *Jeb*-yuh-sites. |
| Mediterranean | *Med*-uh-tuh-***ray***-nee-un. |
| Midianites | *Mid*-ee-un-ites. |
| Miriam | *Meer*-ee-um. |
| patriarchs | *pay*-tree-arks. |
| Perizzites | *Pair*-ih-zites. |
| Pharaoh | *Fair*-o or *Fay*-roe. |
| Rephaims | *Ref*-a-ims. |
| Yahweh *(Hebrew)* | *Yah*-weh. |

(Exodus 2:11-15). Even though a new king sits on the throne (2:23), it is always the wrong time (by human thinking) to ask a powerful king to release his most productive labor force!

*What Do You Think?*

When was a time you moved from saying, "Somebody needs to do this" to "I need to do this"? What motivates us to make this shift?

*Talking Points for Your Discussion*

- Urgency of the need
- Plea from a significant source
- Intersection of need and personal abilities

## II. God Explains

(Exodus 3:11-15)

### A. Doubt and Assurance (vv. 11, 12)

**11. And Moses said unto God, Who am I, that I should go unto Pharaoh, and that I should bring forth the children of Israel out of Egypt?**

Like prophets after him, Moses is reluctant to be God's spokesman. Hundreds of years later, Isaiah will voice his awareness of his own moral impurity (Isaiah 6:5), and Jeremiah will claim to be too young for the job (Jeremiah 1:6). From our perspective, Moses may seem like the perfect candidate. As one who grew up around palace circles (Exodus 2:10), he speaks the language and is acquainted with royal customs. At the very least, his education surpasses that of most of the Israelites of his day (Acts 7:22).

But Moses doesn't seem to see it that way. From his perspective, he is a misfit. We can imagine him thinking that the "purebred" Egyptians look down on him for his Israelite origins. The Israelites, on the other hand, may be suspicious of him for his past connections with their oppressors. When Moses killed a slave driver who was abusing an Israelite, his Egyptian connections were not strong enough to protect him from Pharaoh's wrath, and Moses' Hebrew affiliation was too weak to gain him a sympathetic reception from the very people he was trying to defend (Exodus 2:11-15; Acts 7:24-26).

In addition to all that, Moses is now age 80 (Exodus 7:7), and it has been 40 years since he has been in Egypt (Acts 7:23, 30). Having found a stable home where he is both welcome and trusted, God now is calling him to leave it all behind and march defiantly into the heart of the Egyptian empire! It is little wonder, then, that the elderly Moses deems himself unfit for this mission.

*What Do You Think?*

When was a time you hesitated in your response to a perceived call from God? What contributed to your ultimate decision, right or wrong?

*Talking Points for Your Discussion*

- Becoming aware of God's bigger plan (Acts 10:9-20, 34, 35)
- Focusing on the personal danger (Esther 4:11)
- Seeing the need (Nehemiah 1:1–2:5)
- Other

### *Reluctant to Serve*

Civil war ravaged the West African nation of Liberia from 1989 to 1996. Factions fought one another for seven years, killing 200,000 people and sending 1,000,000 refugees packing. The end of the war did see the end of oppression, however. Finally, in 2005, the "most free, fair and peaceful elections in Liberia's history" brought Ellen Johnson Sirleaf into office as the first democratically elected female president in Africa. She was a reluctant public servant, but nevertheless she provided a stability to the nation that her power-hungry predecessors had not.

Some people look for every opportunity to grab power (see 2 Samuel 15; 1 Kings 1). Others, like Moses, avoid—even outright resist—such opportunities. The key issue in both cases is *motive.* Do we seek power only to enrich ourselves and stroke our egos? Do we avoid such opportunities because of a preference for our current comfort zone? Throughout history, people have responded properly to God's call to serve as leaders. When God calls, be prepared to answer! —C. R. B.

**12. And he said, Certainly I will be with thee; and this shall be a token unto thee, that I have sent thee: When thou hast brought forth the people out of Egypt, ye shall serve God upon this mountain.**

Visual for Lesson 10

*Point to this visual as you ask, "When did you first discover the truth of this statement personally?"*

God is unconcerned with self-doubts. The reason: the Israelites' release is not going to be won on the basis of Moses' diplomatic skills. It is going to be won with a show of God's power. All God needs is a willing messenger. Once Moses adjusts to God's reality, Moses will fit that bill perfectly.

The nature of God's token or sign is worth noting. When humans ask for signs, we often want something like a down payment as to the outcome that is being promised. We want a demonstration of power that is sufficient to convince us that the other party can be trusted to deliver on the promise. Yet God is not like us. Here the sign that He will deliver what He promises will be His fulfillment of the promise. It is as if God is saying to Moses, "Do you doubt that I can pull off the release of your people? You will see it for yourself when they are worshipping me on the very ground on which you are now standing!"

### B. Question and Answer (vv. 13-15)

**13. And Moses said unto God, Behold, when I come unto the children of Israel, and shall say unto them, The God of your fathers hath sent me unto you; and they shall say to me, What is his name? what shall I say unto them?**

The questions that Moses asks are valid from a human standpoint. When a potentially life-changing (and life-threatening) opportunity is placed before us, we want to know who stands behind the opportunity. If we are being asked to step out and take a significant risk, the promise of a nameless benefactor is usually not enough for us.

Yet the request we see here is more difficult than Moses realizes. The God of Israel is not like the fictitious gods that the world concocts—gods with names, addresses, shapes, and fickle personalities that Moses knew of during his time in Egypt. So God needs to change Moses' perspective. As God does so, He will lay a right foundation for His people to understand His sovereign transcendence.

*What Do You Think?*

How do we know when it's time to move from questioning and planning to action in the service of God?

*Talking Points for Your Discussion*

- Valid questions vs. questions of doubt
- Gathering data vs. overanalyzing
- Getting counsel vs. stalling
- Taking responsibility vs. taking the easy way
- Other

**14. And God said unto Moses, I AM THAT I AM: and he said, Thus shalt thou say unto the children of Israel, I AM hath sent me unto you.**

God's self-identification *I AM THAT I AM* includes the ideas of God "who is what He is" and "who will be who He will be" (compare Revelation 1:4, 8; 4:8). This self-identification does not allow the hearer to draw on a prior frame of reference that will fall short of who God is. God is not the best of human experience taken to the nth degree. He is unlike any other being that we might name or experience that we might have.

For this reason, it is crucial that the Christian understanding of God begins with God's self-revelation in Scripture, especially as seen in Jesus (John 8:58). To build doctrine on any other foundation leads to idolatry, regardless of best intentions.

**15. And God said moreover unto Moses, Thus shalt thou say unto the children of Israel, the LORD God of your fathers, the God of Abraham, the God of Isaac, and the God of Jacob, hath sent me unto you: this is my name for ever, and this is my memorial unto all generations.**

God takes two steps further. First, he gives Moses a shorthand way of saying the "I AM

THAT I AM" of verse 14 by providing the name *the Lord* or "Yahweh" (which is our best approximation). This word is built on the same root Hebrew word that comes across in English as "I AM THAT I AM." God reveals His personal divine name to Moses in this verse.

Second, God makes it clear that He will not be known only by what He does in the future (Exodus 3:12), but also by what He began to reveal of himself by His actions to the Israelites' forefathers Abraham, Isaac, and Jacob. God's self-revelation to enslaved Israel will be consistent with His prior self-disclosure to those three patriarchs.

## III. God Sends

(Exodus 3:16, 17)

### A. Elders Assembled (v. 16)

**16. Go, and gather the elders of Israel together, and say unto them, The LORD God of your fathers, the God of Abraham, of Isaac, and of Jacob, appeared unto me, saying, I have surely visited you, and seen that which is done to you in Egypt.**

Before God sends Moses to Pharaoh, He sends Moses to his own people. They stand in a privileged relationship of knowledge of God's plans (compare Amos 3:7). Moses will visit Pharaoh soon enough, but God's people must first get on board with the plan. Their first reception of His message is quite positive according to Exodus 4:29-31.

*What Do You Think?*

Without direct communication from God such as Moses received, how do you discern what God is calling you to do?

*Talking Points for Your Discussion*

- Holy Spirit guidance
- Spiritual giftedness
- Closed and opened doors of opportunity
- Counsel by fellow Christians
- Other

### B. Plan Announced (v. 17)

**17. And I have said, I will bring you up out of the affliction of Egypt unto the land of the Canaanites, and the Hittites, and the Amorites, and the Perizzites, and the Hivites, and the Jebusites, unto a land flowing with milk and honey.**

The six groups listed here (as well as v. 8, above) are small tribes that occupy various plots of land in Canaan. They are never as powerful as Israel is in the days of David and Solomon, so they are easily controlled by stronger nations around them. These groups are named in various passages throughout the Old Testament, but especially Exodus through Joshua. In some passages, the Girgashites, Kenites, Kadmonites, and Rephaims are also listed (example: Genesis 15:20, 21; see commentary on this passage in lesson 6); in other places, the Hivites are left out (example: Nehemiah 9:8); and in still other places, just one or a few are named to represent the grouping (example: Genesis 15:16).

Because of Israel's failure to obey God fully, these six people groups remain in the land after the Israelites settle into it (Judges 3:5). They are still there during Solomon's day (2 Chronicles 8:7). Regarding *a land flowing with milk and honey,* see commentary on Exodus 3:8, above.

## Conclusion

### A. Servant of God

Though we cannot be sure what Moses' life was like as an adopted son of Pharaoh's daughter, we know what it was like after God laid claim to him. Moses learned that the holy God sees and hears, that God's power is all that is needed to accomplish God's mission, that God's name is unlike any other name, and that God's people have an important role to play in His plans. We who would continue to serve this God by seeking first His kingdom must take to heart these lessons!

### B. Prayer

Lord God, we, like Moses, come before You with doubt that we are fit to be used of You to accomplish anything of lasting value for the world. Please prove us wrong! In Jesus' name, amen.

### C. Thought to Remember

Join God in delivering people from sin-slavery.

# Involvement Learning

*Some of the activities below are also found in the helpful student book,* Adult Bible Class. *Don't forget to download the free reproducible page from www.standardlesson.com to enhance your lesson!*

## Into the Lesson

Have on display this question: *What's in a name?* Have five learners ready to read these quotes regarding names, one each: (1) "The name of a man is a numbing blow from which he never recovers" (Marshall McLuhan); (2) "That which we call a rose, by any other name would smell as sweet" (William Shakespeare, in *Romeo and Juliet*); (3) "Tigers die and leave their skins; people die and leave their names" (Japanese proverb); (4) "Proper names are poetry in the raw. Like all poetry they are untranslatable" (W. H. Auden); (5) "A good name is rather to be chosen than great riches" (Proverbs 22:1). Learners may wish to comment on these ideas as each is presented. Note that today's study revolves around a "name question."

## Into the Word

Prepare in advance 16 blank dialogue balloons (typical of comic strips) cut from 8½" x 11" sheets of white paper. Say, "In today's text we are privileged to overhear a very personal conversation. I have a collection of dialogue balloons to help us get a handle on this." Distribute the dialogue balloons and markers; if your class is small, give two or more to some learners. Then assign from Exodus 3 these verses: 3, 4a, 4b, 5, 6, 7, 8, 9, 10, 11, 12, 13, 14, 15, 16, 17. Do not assign back-to-back verses to the learners having more than one dialogue balloon. (Verses 3-6 are not part of today's printed text, but are an important part of the conversation.)

Say, "In as few words as possible, summarize what the speaker says in your assigned verse(s). When you finish, give your balloon(s) to me." After all are submitted, shuffle them. Comment: "Now we have a jumbled conversation, so I need your help in reassembling the ideas. As I read a quote, tell me if it is early, middle, or late in the conversation, and I will post it accordingly. Close your Bibles!"

Read a dialogue balloon, receive responses, and affix the dialogue balloon to the wall or board with masking tape. Repeat for all. When you finish, ask learners if the arrangement looks proper for representing the sequence of the text. If they do not think so, ask, "How should this be fixed?" Rearrange as necessary.

*Option.* You can note that this is one of the longest recorded conversations between God and a person in the Scriptures. Ask if learners can recall other long conversations. For each identified, ask, "What would you say is the key issue involved?" One example is God and Isaiah in Isaiah 6; the issue (similar to this one in Exodus 3) is Isaiah's becoming God's spokesperson to His people.

## Into Life

*Option:* For a transition to this segment, distribute copies of the "Talking with God" activity from the reproducible page, which you can download. Ask learners to summarize God's conversation with Moses using only the two dialogue balloons, then complete the bottom half of the exercise as indicated. Ask for volunteers to reveal responses.

Say, "Broadly speaking, there are two types of oppressions today: physical and spiritual. Who are some of the cruel taskmasters of each?" Let learners respond freely. In the *physical oppression* area, learners may mention dictators, those involved in human trafficking, etc.; if someone mentions "government policy," be careful not to allow the discussion to drift into one of partisan politics. The obvious answer in the *spiritual oppression* area is Satan, but learners may also mention some of his human ambassadors.

As the list grows, ask simply, "How do you see yourself as a deliverer for those oppressed by such powers?" Ask also, "What, if anything, can our class do corporately?"

*Alternative:* Distribute copies of the "Oppression and Deliverance" activity from the reproducible page. This exercise poses similar questions, but with more focus on Scripture background.

# Beginning of Passover

**Devotional Reading:** John 1:29-37
**Background Scripture:** Exodus 6:2-30; 12

## Exodus 12:1-14

**1 And the LORD spake unto Moses and Aaron in the land of Egypt, saying,**

**2 This month shall be unto you the beginning of months: it shall be the first month of the year to you.**

**3 Speak ye unto all the congregation of Israel, saying, In the tenth day of this month they shall take to them every man a lamb, according to the house of their fathers, a lamb for an house:**

**4 And if the household be too little for the lamb, let him and his neighbour next unto his house take it according to the number of the souls; every man according to his eating shall make your count for the lamb.**

**5 Your lamb shall be without blemish, a male of the first year: ye shall take it out from the sheep, or from the goats:**

**6 And ye shall keep it up until the fourteenth day of the same month: and the whole assembly of the congregation of Israel shall kill it in the evening.**

**7 And they shall take of the blood, and strike it on the two side posts and on the upper door post of the houses, wherein they shall eat it.**

**8 And they shall eat the flesh in that night, roast with fire, and unleavened bread; and with bitter herbs they shall eat it.**

**9 Eat not of it raw, nor sodden at all with water, but roast with fire; his head with his legs, and with the purtenance thereof.**

**10 And ye shall let nothing of it remain until the morning; and that which remaineth of it until the morning ye shall burn with fire.**

**11 And thus shall ye eat it; with your loins girded, your shoes on your feet, and your staff in your hand; and ye shall eat it in haste: it is the LORD's passover.**

**12 For I will pass through the land of Egypt this night, and will smite all the firstborn in the land of Egypt, both man and beast; and against all the gods of Egypt I will execute judgment: I am the LORD.**

**13 And the blood shall be to you for a token upon the houses where ye are: and when I see the blood, I will pass over you, and the plague shall not be upon you to destroy you, when I smite the land of Egypt.**

**14 And this day shall be unto you for a memorial; and ye shall keep it a feast to the LORD throughout your generations; ye shall keep it a feast by an ordinance for ever.**

## Key Verse

*This day shall be unto you for a memorial; and ye shall keep it a feast to the LORD throughout your generations; ye shall keep it a feast by an ordinance for ever.* —**Exodus 12:14**

# FIRST THINGS

## Unit 3: First Freedom

LESSONS 10–13

## LESSON AIMS

After participating in this lesson, each student will be able to:

1. Recall the details of the first Passover, just before the Israelites left Egypt.

2. Explain the importance of keeping alive the memory of events that have spiritual significance.

3. Brainstorm ways to make the "visual aids" of baptism and the Lord's Supper more meaningful in his or her church.

## LESSON OUTLINE

Introduction
- A. A Beginning to Remember
- B. Lesson Background

I. When to Eat the Lamb (EXODUS 12:1-7)
- A. The First Month (vv. 1, 2)
- B. The Tenth Day (vv. 3-5)
- C. The Fourteenth Day (vv. 6, 7)

II. How to Eat the Lamb (EXODUS 12:8-11)
- A. Proper Action (vv. 8-10)
  - *Learning to Cook*
- B. Proper Attire (v. 11)
  - *No Hurry?*

III. Why to Eat the Lamb (EXODUS 12:12-14)
- A. Passing Through (v. 12)
- B. Passing Over (v. 13)
- C. Passing On (v. 14)

Conclusion
- A. An Unforgettable Ending
- B. Prayer
- C. Thought to Remember

## Introduction

### A. A Beginning to Remember

People like to remember how things began. Nations celebrate their origins with holidays, solemn ceremonies, and raucous parades. Families celebrate marriages and the anniversaries that follow with parties, gifts, and cakes. Organizations celebrate their founding with employee picnics, commemorative products, and contests.

We need to celebrate important events because it is all too easy to forget what has brought us to the point where we are now. "The daily grind" may consume our time and energy to the point that unless we plan to slow down and contemplate what is important, we will not say the "deeper" things that need to be said, think what needs to be thought, and do what needs to be done. Important people and historic moments will fade from memory as we forget what made them special.

Forgetfulness can lead to disaster as mistakes are repeated and purposes (reasons for being) are lost. The meaning of life can get swallowed up by life's demands; the direction God has given world history can be replaced with a pointless, repetitive cycle.

God knows the importance of remembering beginnings. He gave the ancient Israelites three practices by which to remember their founding event, the exodus from Egypt: (1) the rite of the firstborn son, (2) the meal of unleavened bread, and (3) the celebration of the Passover feast. Today's lesson focuses on the third of these.

### B. Lesson Background

The Passover feast, like other commemorations, must be considered within the historical context in which it occurred. Further, we must look not just to the immediate context, but also to the larger context of history for fullest comprehension.

For Passover, that context goes all the way back to Genesis 1. In the first 11 chapters of Genesis, we see God's good creation collapsing under the weight of human sinfulness. Not even the catastrophic event of the great flood could cure what ailed the world. Rather than forsake humanity, however, God formed a people through whom

He would bless all nations. They would be His vehicle for ushering in the Messiah to reconcile a wounded world to Him.

This people began with Abraham and Sarah. Generations later, the growing nation of their descendants found itself enslaved within the confines of Egyptian civilization. Pharaoh, feeling threatened by their growth, suppressed them with harsh toil and deadly population control. After centuries of progressively worse treatment, the cries of the Hebrews moved God to action. He raised up a figure who would lead the Israelites out of Egypt as God willed to develop them as a light to the nations.

Moses was that leader. Through Moses, God unleashed a barrage of plagues against the Egyptians. These plagues eventually broke Pharaoh's stubborn will, but he has not yet conceded defeat as today's text begins. In anticipation of the tenth and final plague, God established the Passover instructions as specified in today's text. By these, generations of Israelites were to remember their exemption from the associated catastrophe (Exodus 12:24-27).

## I. When to Eat the Lamb

(Exodus 12:1-7)

### A. The First Month (vv. 1, 2)

**1, 2. And the Lord spake unto Moses and Aaron in the land of Egypt, saying, This month shall be unto you the beginning of months: it shall be the first month of the year to you.**

Having shocked Egypt with nine devastating plagues to this point, God is on the verge of delivering His people from their oppressors. From God's perspective, the "what for" of this deliverance matters more than the "what from." God is not liberating all oppressed peoples throughout the world; He is liberating a specific group of slaves for His mission of forming a new people that He will use to bless all nations.

If the Hebrew people are to bless the nations, they will need to live differently from their oppressors. To become a light, they will have to exhibit a life rhythm different from that of the Egyptians. One feature of this new rhythm is a distinctive calendar. Since (1) deliverance from Egypt marks the founding moment in Israel's national history and (2) the Passover is the most important event to mark this deliverance, then (3) God decrees that this observance should occur in the month that is to mark the beginning of Israel's new year. This observance therefore takes place in the month of Abib (Exodus 13:4), later called Nisan (Esther 3:7).

*What Do You Think?*

What are some ways that Christians are to "live differently" from unbelievers? How will you improve in this regard?

*Talking Points for Your Discussion*

- Regarding church involvement
- Regarding family life
- Regarding ethical standards
- Regarding compassion
- Ephesians 4:17–5:20

### B. The Tenth Day (vv. 3-5)

**3. Speak ye unto all the congregation of Israel, saying, In the tenth day of this month they shall take to them every man a lamb, according to the house of their fathers, a lamb for an house.**

God's calendar for Israel is populated with special months and days. A key pattern in this calendar is the use of significant numbers, especially 10 and multiples of 7. The number 10 corresponds both to the number of plagues God sends on Egypt and the number of commandments He gives Israel (Exodus 20). It is fitting, then, that God instructs His people to begin preparation for Passover on *the tenth day* of the first month of

## HOW TO SAY IT

| | |
|---|---|
| Abib | *A*-bib. |
| Abraham | *Ay*-bruh-ham. |
| Levites | *Lee*-vites. |
| Messiah | Meh-*sigh*-uh. |
| Nisan | *Nye*-san. |
| Pharaoh | *Fair*-o or *Fay*-roe. |
| purtenance | *purt*-nunts. |

their year. On this day, one man in each house is required to select a lamb. The emphasis here is that God's requirement applies to every household.

**4. And if the household be too little for the lamb, let him and his neighbour next unto his house take it according to the number of the souls; every man according to his eating shall make your count for the lamb.**

God recognizes that not all households are equally blessed in numbers of people and financial resources. It is crucial, however, that the smaller and/or poorer households not be excluded from Israel's shared life. God therefore allows—and requires—households to combine resources so that all may participate. Everyone must join in if this practice is to have the desired effect of uniting God's people according to their common history and mission.

*What Do You Think?*

With Thanksgiving approaching, what can you do to include a "little" household in your own celebration of thanks to God?

*Talking Points for Your Discussion*

- Regarding widows, widowers, and other singles
- Regarding a homeless person
- Regarding stranded travelers (bad weather, hospital emergency room, etc.)
- Other

**5. Your lamb shall be without blemish, a male of the first year: ye shall take it out from the sheep, or from the goats.**

Not just any animal may be selected for the Passover meal. The animal must *be without blemish,* as with all sacrifices in Israel's worship life that God will establish later (compare Exodus 29:1; Leviticus 22:21; Numbers 19:2; etc.). To offer an animal with a defect would communicate that this practice is not very important (see Malachi 1:8, 12-14). The Israelites must offer their best because their God is the best thing that has ever happened to them!

The animal must also be *a male of the first year.* Its gender may represent Israel's firstborn sons, who are to be spared the tenth plague—the plague that will take the lives of Egypt's firstborn males (Exodus 11:5; 12:29, 30). The lamb's young age may represent Israel's youthful vigor as a nation.

It is not essential that the animal to be sacrificed be a sheep, which is what we normally associate with the word *lamb.* A young goat will do just as well. God recognizes that not all households have access to both, so He leaves the option open.

### C. The Fourteenth Day (vv. 6, 7)

**6. And ye shall keep it up until the fourteenth day of the same month: and the whole assembly of the congregation of Israel shall kill it in the evening.**

Four days after selecting the lambs, the households within Israel must slaughter them. The time appointed for this, *in the evening,* is after the sun begins to set but before darkness falls completely. Responsibility for slaughtering the animals transfers eventually from heads of households to Levites and/or priests as time passes (2 Chronicles 35:1-11; Ezra 6:20).

**7. And they shall take of the blood, and strike it on the two side posts and on the upper door post of the houses, wherein they shall eat it.**

The purpose for smearing blood on the doorposts is discussed in verse 13, below. This practice and that of eating inside one's house are not permanent features of this feast. After the Israelites settle into the promised land, the celebration will be centralized in "the place which the Lord thy God shall choose to place his name in" (Deuteronomy 16:6).

## II. How to Eat the Lamb

(Exodus 12:8-11)

### A. Proper Action (vv. 8-10)

**8a. And they shall eat the flesh in that night, roast with fire,**

The fact that the people are to *eat the flesh in that night* implies haste in the preparation of the Passover lamb. There is no time for marinating the meat extensively. The symbolic value of this practice requires that it be eaten hastily (see v. 11).

**8b. And unleavened bread;**

The "haste factor" also applies to the bread of the meal. Leavened bread (that is, bread made with yeast) requires time to rise. But there will not be enough time for such a process because the Israelites will have only a narrow window of time to depart after God strikes Egypt with the final plague. The people must be ready to go.

**8c. And with bitter herbs they shall eat it.**

The use of *bitter herbs* points to the bitterness of Israel's oppression in Egypt (Exodus 1:14; Numbers 9:11). Lettuce and endive are the most common bitter herbs that are native to the region.

*What Do You Think?*

Is it appropriate for Christians to remind themselves periodically of the bitterness of their lives while slaves to sin? Why, or why not?

*Talking Points for Your Discussion*

- Rejoicing in deliverance (Romans 5:11)
- Feeling overwhelmed with regret (1 Corinthians 15:9)

**9. Eat not of it raw, nor sodden at all with water, but roast with fire; his head with his legs, and with the purtenance thereof.**

The meat must be prepared properly. God makes clear in Genesis 9:4 that all lifeblood is sacred to Him (see lesson 4). For this reason, the people must not eat meat that has blood still in it. The people must drain all blood, effectively returning it to the author of life. God will stress this repeatedly after the exodus (Deuteronomy 12:16, 23-25; 15:23). In the instructions in Leviticus 17:10-13 (which the Israelites have not received at this point), God even will require that blood poured onto the ground be covered with dust (contrast Ezekiel 24:7).

Roasting animals is one way to make sure that no blood remains. Meat that is consumed raw or after having been boiled *(sodden . . . with water)* is much more likely to have blood still in it. *Purtenance* refers to the inner organs (compare Exodus 29:13, 17, 22).

### *Learning to Cook*

Would you like to be a great chef? The Internet offers many descriptions of self-proclaimed "world-class" cooking schools. One such institution in New York proclaims itself to be "the best culinary school in the world." It boasts that its students spend in excess of 1,300 hours in the kitchen or bakeshop. Offered are degrees for professionals and certificates for those who are merely "food enthusiasts." Do you suppose that includes those of us who just like to eat?

Visual for Lesson 11. *Use this visual to start a discussion regarding the connection between Passover and Christ's sacrifice.*

A cooking school in California asserts that its name "is synonymous with expertise, refinement, and culinary excellence—qualities meticulously nurtured" in its programs. A school in Chicago that specializes in French pastry boasts that it provides "an intense focus on contemporary aesthetics." Wouldn't most of us rather eat a pastry than merely stare at it?

Kidding aside, what the Hebrew cooks prepared on the evening of the Passover had to be done quickly; there was no time for culinary-school aesthetics and refinement. It was God's recipe that had to be followed for that simple meal. And so it is with God's other "recipes" as seen in, for example, Matthew 28:19, 20; John 3:36; Acts 2:38; and James 1:6. Don't try to "improve" God's recipes—just follow them in faith! —C. R. B.

**10. And ye shall let nothing of it remain until the morning; and that which remaineth of it until the morning ye shall burn with fire.**

The practice of completely burning the sacrificial lamb anticipates two features of Israel's future practices of eating and sacrificing. First, it anticipates the eating of manna (Exodus 16:11-36). As the Israelites journey toward the promised land, God will provide food by raining down manna from Heaven. Yet God will insist that the Israelites collect only enough manna to eat each day. With one exception (see Exodus 16:21-23), nothing shall remain for future consumption. This practice will remind the Israelites of their dependence on God for their daily bread. In destroying the leftovers of the Passover feast, the people will learn that God is the source of their sustenance. We echo this lesson when we ask our heavenly Father to give us our daily bread (Matthew 6:11).

Second, the Israelites acknowledge the sacredness of the meal by ensuring that the animal is entirely consumed by the combination of eating and burning. The meat may not be used partially for a sacred feast on one day with leftovers being used the next day to feed livestock or to serve as an afternoon snack. It is sacred food. This will be the imagery of the burnt offerings of Israel's forthcoming sacrificial system (Leviticus 1:1-9).

### B. Proper Attire (v. 11)

**11. And thus shall ye eat it; with your loins girded, your shoes on your feet, and your staff in your hand; and ye shall eat it in haste: it is the LORD's passover.**

The command to have *your loins girded, your shoes on your feet, and your staff in your hand* speaks not only to behavior, but also to the attitude the people are to have as they prepare to head onward in faith. Once the Passover meal is eaten, there is to be no hesitation as with Lot's wife (Genesis 19:26). The attire God specifies is dress for the road (compare Luke 12:35).

*What Do You Think?*

In what ways can and should Sunday morning worship prepare us to be "ready to go" for service to God?

*Talking Points for Your Discussion*

- The role of the sermon
- The role of the Lord's Supper
- The role of Christian fellowship
- The role of corporate prayer
- Other

### *No Hurry?*

Even after slavery was outlawed in America in the 1860s, the de facto law of the land in parts of the U.S. continued to limit the freedoms of former slaves and their descendants. The U.S. Supreme Court decision Plessy v. Ferguson of 1896 made things worse by upholding a "separate but equal" law, which permitted continued segregation.

This situation took a dramatic turn in 1954. That was the year of the landmark Brown v. Board of Education of Topeka decision in which the U.S. Supreme Court overturned Plessy v. Ferguson. The civil rights movement of the 1960s followed.

Thomas Jefferson, himself a slave owner, had penned the words "all men are created equal" for the U.S. Declaration of Independence in 1776. Looking back from our vantage point in the year 2013, we wonder why it took so long to put into practice the truth of that statement! Patience is often a virtue (Psalms 37:7; 40:1). But "taking our time" is sinful when we delay making changes that we know we should.

God is patient and longsuffering (Romans 9:22; 1 Peter 3:20). But the Bible also shows God acting quickly and demanding that we do so as well. It was so on the night of the Passover, and it is so today as God calls us to a new life in Jesus, a life free from the slavery of sin. There should be no delay. "How shall we, that are dead to sin, live any longer therein?" (Romans 6:2). —C. R. B.

## III. Why to Eat the Lamb

(EXODUS 12:12-14)

### A. Passing Through (v. 12)

**12. For I will pass through the land of Egypt this night, and will smite all the firstborn in the land of Egypt, both man and beast; and against all the gods of Egypt I will execute judgment: I am the LORD.**

Time after time, the hardness of Pharaoh's heart kept him from releasing God's people. So God is about to inflict a strict judgment on Pharaoh and his people. As God's chosen people, Israel is God's firstborn (Exodus 4:22), the people to whom He is entrusting the responsibility of carrying His legacy. If Pharaoh refuses to honor God's exclusive claim on His firstborn, then Pharaoh and his people will have to forfeit *their* firstborn.

There also may be a tie-in with Pharaoh's decision to kill all newborn Israelite boys (Exodus 1:16). By taking the life of only the firstborn of Egypt, God is not giving Pharaoh the equal measure he deserves. Nevertheless, God is about to send a powerful message to Pharaoh that he has no rightful claim on the lives of God's people. For Pharaoh to kill every Hebrew newborn boy is an act of genocide since all the Hebrew females eventually would be absorbed into the Egyptian nation. Were that to happen, Abraham's descendants would no longer be distinguishable as a people-group.

### B. Passing Over (v. 13)

**13. And the blood shall be to you for a token upon the houses where ye are: and when I see the blood, I will pass over you, and the plague shall not be upon you to destroy you, when I smite the land of Egypt.**

God does not want to punish the Israelites along with the Egyptians. So He uses the lambs' blood that is smeared on the doorposts (v. 7, above) as the distinguishing mark regarding who shall live. In anticipation of Jesus, the lambs' blood is to "cover" God's people, and they will be spared from death. Of course, God does not need the blood to tell who is who. But the Israelites need to learn to follow God's instructions since they are in the process of becoming His set-apart people.

### C. Passing On (v. 14)

**14. And this day shall be unto you for a memorial; and ye shall keep it a feast to the LORD throughout your generations; ye shall keep it a feast by an ordinance for ever.**

The lessons God is teaching the Israelites through the Passover event are relevant to future generations. If the lessons are not to be forgotten, then God's people will have to instill them into each subsequent generation (compare Deuteronomy 6:20-25). This is the purpose of the meal. It is to serve as a permanent fixture in the calendar of Old Testament Israel. As the Israelites continue to observe Passover, their children will not forget who they are, where they came from, and where they are going as God's chosen people.

> *What Do You Think?*
>
> What traditions can we establish in our family celebrations to pass along spiritual truths to children and grandchildren?
>
> *Talking Points for Your Discussion*
>
> - Regarding Thanksgiving
> - Regarding Christmas
> - Regarding Easter
> - Regarding birthdays

## Conclusion

### A. An Unforgettable Ending

People may try to avoid remembering how certain things come to an end (jobs, marriages, the lives of loved ones, etc.). Endings tend to be sad because we do not like to let go. We do not like the instability that the end of something familiar brings into our lives. An ending of something often signals entrance into the unknown as comfortable routines must be abandoned and new ones developed.

Yet endings sometimes are gateways to new beginnings that far outshine the past. The Passover was just such a gateway. In this vein, Christ has given us the Lord's Supper for us to remember the end of Jesus' earthly life that leads to resurrection life in Him. The facts surrounding the ending of Jesus' earthly ministry belong in our memory because they are the foundation of our new life in Him. It is thus fitting that Jesus instituted the Lord's Supper in the context of the Passover meal. Remembering what Jesus has done is a vital foundation to being able to "teach all nations" as Jesus would have us do (Matthew 28:19).

### B. Prayer

Thank You, God, for new beginnings! As we think of Passover, let us not forget the new beginning You brought by sending Your spotless lamb, Jesus, to die on our behalf. In His name, amen.

### C. Thought to Remember

God's deliverance is always there for us.

# Involvement Learning

*Some of the activities below are also found in the helpful student book,* Adult Bible Class. *Don't forget to download the free reproducible page from www.standardlesson.com to enhance your lesson!*

## Into the Lesson

*Option:* Place in chairs copies of the "Egyptians Fall, Part 1" exercise from the reproducible page, which you can download. Learners can begin working on this as they arrive. (*Alternative:* Distribute this at the end of class as a take-home activity.)

Prepare a 2014 calendar that fits on a single 8½" by 11" sheet of paper. (Search for "calendar template" on the Internet.) Give each learner a copy. Also bring a full-color decorative calendar to hang before the group. Say, "Circle what you consider to be 'special days' in the coming year." Allow two or three minutes, then ask, "Who has a special day marked in January?" Continue naming the remaining 11 months as your class members raise hands in response. (Keep this moving rapidly; you want only shows of hands, not discussions of which days are special and why.)

Comment: "Wow—that's a lot of special days! Some of those are important personally; others involve family members; still others involve larger groups, such as our church as a whole. Each special day has its own significance. Today's study is about one of the most significant days on the calendar of Old Testament Israel—it's Passover."

## Into the Word

Distribute handouts with *Time to* printed across the top; have the word *REMEMBER* vertically down the middle of the page. (*Alternative:* Distribute blank sheets of paper and have learners write these words themselves, in the desired arrangement.) Read the lesson text read aloud, then say, "Close your Bibles for a memory test! I'm going to ask some questions and give some completion statements. We are going to work down through the eight letters of the word *remember* in sequence. Jot each one-word answer so that it intersects with the letter under consideration. Here goes."

*R:* How was the lamb to be cooked? *(roasted, v. 9); E:* What part of the meal was to be bitter? *(herbs, v. 8); M:* Leftover meat was to be burned before what time of day? *(morning, v. 10); E:* On which day of the month was the lamb to be taken and set aside? *(tenth, v. 3); M:* What was declared to be "the first"? *(month, v. 2); B:* What was to be put on doorposts? *(blood, v. 7); E:* In what manner was the meal to be eaten? *(haste, v. 11); R:* Other than Moses, to whom was the Lord speaking? *(Aaron, v. 1).*

Discuss results and review the Scripture text to correct any misconceptions or deficiencies.

Note that Passover was about a new way to worship God for Old Testament Israel in celebration of a salvation event. Ask simply, "What do you see that is 'new' in today's text?" Expect learners to point out the new calendar and a new observance (Passover) on that calendar; learners may then point out more "newnesses" in relation to those two: a new use of blood; a new spirit of community inclusion, etc. Continue: "Which Passover elements are given new significance for us as we observe the Lord's Supper? Why?" (See 1 Corinthians 11:23-25.)

## Into Life

Launch a brainstorming session as you say, "The procedures of the Passover celebration result in 'visual aids' to make the feast meaningful and memorable to succeeding generations. What can we do to make the Lord's Supper and baptism more meaningful in terms of the 'visual aids' that they provide for us?" (*Option:* Divide the class in half, one to discuss the Lord's Supper in this regard and one to discuss baptism.)

*Option:* Distribute copies of the "A New Day, A New Way" activity from the reproducible page. Ask a learner to read 1 Corinthians 5:7 aloud. Use this text to launch a discussion of attitudes, speech, and behaviors that are sinful "leaven." Learners can use the cutout of the exercise as a memory tool in the week ahead, as noted.

November 17
Lesson 12

# Beginning of Freedom

**Devotional Reading:** Galatians 5:13-21
**Background Scripture:** Exodus 13:17-22; 14

## Exodus 14:13, 14, 21-30

**13 And Moses said unto the people, Fear ye not, stand still, and see the salvation of the Lord, which he will shew to you to day: for the Egyptians whom ye have seen to day, ye shall see them again no more for ever.**

**14 The Lord shall fight for you, and ye shall hold your peace.**

. . . . . . . . . . . . . . . . . . . . . . . . .

**21 And Moses stretched out his hand over the sea; and the Lord caused the sea to go back by a strong east wind all that night, and made the sea dry land, and the waters were divided.**

**22 And the children of Israel went into the midst of the sea upon the dry ground: and the waters were a wall unto them on their right hand, and on their left.**

**23 And the Egyptians pursued, and went in after them to the midst of the sea, even all Pharaoh's horses, his chariots, and his horsemen.**

**24 And it came to pass, that in the morning watch the Lord looked unto the host of the Egyptians through the pillar of fire and of the cloud, and troubled the host of the Egyptians,**

**25 And took off their chariot wheels, that they drave them heavily: so that the Egyptians said, Let us flee from the face of Israel; for the Lord fighteth for them against the Egyptians.**

**26 And the Lord said unto Moses, Stretch out thine hand over the sea, that the waters may come again upon the Egyptians, upon their chariots, and upon their horsemen.**

**27 And Moses stretched forth his hand over the sea, and the sea returned to his strength when the morning appeared; and the Egyptians fled against it; and the Lord overthrew the Egyptians in the midst of the sea.**

**28 And the waters returned, and covered the chariots, and the horsemen, and all the host of Pharaoh that came into the sea after them; there remained not so much as one of them.**

**29 But the children of Israel walked upon dry land in the midst of the sea; and the waters were a wall unto them on their right hand, and on their left.**

**30 Thus the Lord saved Israel that day out of the hand of the Egyptians; and Israel saw the Egyptians dead upon the sea shore.**

## Key Verse

*Thus the Lord saved Israel that day out of the hand of the Egyptians.* **—Exodus 14:30**

# First Things

## Unit 3: First Freedom

Lessons 10–13

## Lesson Aims

After participating in this lesson, each student will be able to:

1. Tell how Israel escaped from Egypt by crossing the Red Sea.

2. Compare and contrast the Israelites' deliverance from bondage through crossing the Red Sea with the role of baptismal water in delivering believers from the bondage of sin (1 Corinthians 10:1, 2).

3. Sing a song of praise to God, giving thanks for salvation.

## Lesson Outline

Introduction
- A. From Despair to Deliverance
- B. Lesson Background

I. Terrifying Situation (Exodus 14:13, 14)
- A. Watch Closely (v. 13)
- B. Do Nothing (v. 14)
  - *The Fight-or-Flight Response*

II. Miraculous Intervention (Exodus 14:21-28)
- A. Israelites Escape (vv. 21, 22)
- B. Egyptians Pursue (v. 23)
- C. God Fights (vv. 24, 25)
- D. Egyptians Perish (vv. 26-28)
  - *Power from Above*

III. Victorious Resolution (Exodus 14:29, 30)
- A. Summary of Deliverance (v. 29)
- B. Evidence of Freedom (v. 30)

Conclusion
- A. Our Great Salvation
- B. Prayer
- C. Thought to Remember

## Introduction

### A. From Despair to Deliverance

We were supposed to fly directly across Lake Michigan and down the Wisconsin coast to Chicago's Midway Airport. However, the storm was so strong we had to hug the shoreline of Michigan, flying south, bumping hard every second. I knew we were in trouble when the businessmen who took this flight daily were visibly frightened. It seemed that the plane would break apart any second. Our seat belts hardly held us in place as we bounced around. There was no way to fly out of it.

After more than an hour with teeth chattering and hearts pounding, we emerged into smooth air just south of the airport. The evening sun was setting, and rays were filtering through the storm clouds. We landed safely, and everyone clapped for joy for the "great salvation" we had just experienced. We had moved quickly from despair to deliverance.

Perhaps our emotions were a bit like what the Israelites experienced at the Red Sea. Their exodus has become a figure of the Christian experience of salvation and freedom from sin.

### B. Lesson Background

To understand the miraculous nature of the exodus events, one must look back to the very beginnings of the book of Exodus itself. In the first place, young Moses was saved from a death sentence by divine circumstances to be reared in Pharaoh's household (Exodus 2:1-10; Acts 7:20-22). But at age 40, Moses killed an Egyptian overseer and had to flee for his own life. He then spent 40 years as a shepherd before being confronted by God in the burning bush (Exodus 2:11–3:22; Acts 7:23-32). Moses thus became the man to lead God's people out of Egypt (Exodus 3–6).

The miracles of the plagues reached a climax with the death of the firstborn in Egypt (Exodus 7–11). When Pharaoh finally let the people go, God did not lead them by a northern route, the most direct way to Canaan (13:17); rather, He led them toward the south "through the way of the wilderness of the Red sea" (13:18). By the time the Israelites "encamped in Etham, in the edge of the wilderness" (13:20), the people had seen many miracles performed by God through Moses. Thus they should have been confident in the outcome of what was coming next.

When we read Exodus 14:2, we see that God had deliberately led the people into an impossible position (from a human point of view), with their backs to the sea. God placed Israel in this position—with no apparent way to escape the Egyptian army—in order that He might show His glory to the Israelites.

An Israelite countermarch tricked Pharaoh into thinking that the Israelites were confused in their attempt to escape into the wilderness (v. 3). God used this opportunity to "harden Pharaoh's heart" so Pharaoh would chase after the Israelites with his army (vv. 4-6). This he did, with his 600 "chosen" chariots plus many other chariots and horsemen (vv. 7-9). The Israelites reacted with great fear and consternation (v. 10). With sarcasm, "they said unto Moses, Because there were no graves in Egypt, hast thou taken us away to die in the wilderness?" (v. 11). Time for another miracle!

## I. Terrifying Situation

(Exodus 14:13, 14)

### A. Watch Closely (v. 13)

**13. And Moses said unto the people, Fear ye not, stand still, and see the salvation of the Lord, which he will shew to you to day: for the Egyptians whom ye have seen to day, ye shall see them again no more for ever.**

Ancient Egypt is a culture obsessed with a religion of death. The pyramids, which are monumental tombs for the Pharaohs, testify to this fact. The pyramids were built long before the time of Moses, and it is against this "religion of death" backdrop that Moses speaks words of encouragement.

The Hebrew word for *stand still* is a special form that means "to take one's stand within oneself." Thus the phrase *stand still* is addressed more to the hearer's attitude than to physical posture. In other words, the Israelites are to be calm and confident, not wavering in their trust in God. All they have to do is wait and *see the salvation of the Lord.*

The word *see,* used three times, is emphasized in this verse. At the end of the chapter, at the conclusion of the great salvation accomplished by God, the Israelites will *see* "Egyptians dead upon the sea shore," they will *see* God's "great work" (Exodus 14:30, 31). Moses addresses the people's fears most appropriately as he predicts that *the Egyptians whom ye have seen to day, ye shall see them again no more for ever.* Death is about to become a sudden reality for many Egyptians, whose culture is fixated on a religion of death.

### B. Do Nothing (v. 14)

**14. The Lord shall fight for you, and ye shall hold your peace.**

The Lord is the "man of war" (Exodus 15:3) who announces His strategy and goals from the beginning (see 6:2-8). The exodus events, wilderness experiences, and conquest of Canaan are and will be God's battle. The Lord has His part in what is about to happen, and the Israelites have theirs: it is to shut up and watch. Unfortunately, the people are beginning to develop the bad habit of running off at the mouth when silence would indicate faith.

*What Do You Think?*

What was the most terrifying experience of your life? How did you grow spiritually as a result?

*Talking Points for Your Discussion*

- Lessons learned about God's power
- Lessons learned about your own tendencies
- Lessons learned about spiritual "blind spots"
- Other

### *The Fight-or-Flight Response*

Stress-filled situations can trigger the fight-or-flight mechanism that seems to be built in to most of God's creatures. The leader (alpha male) of a wolf pack will fight if challenged for leadership. A deer will flee for her life when sensing a predator nearby.

Humans demonstrate the same two responses in stressful situations. God seems to have hard-wired us for either "fight or flight" when danger looms. Many people will flee from a burning building while others remain inside to help others escape. Those fleeing want to save their own lives; those remaining inside are fighting for the lives of loved ones. But no one simply hangs around inside a burning building to see what will happen next!

In anticipation of the Egyptian attack, Moses' commands of "fear ye not," "stand still," and "hold your peace" challenged his people to override their fight-or-flight instinct. They could do so by replacing that instinct with trust in God. The Bible requires that we use godly wisdom as we evaluate situations in this regard. There are indeed times to fight (2 Corinthians 10:3-5; 1 Timothy 6:12; etc.) and circumstances to flee (Acts 9:23-25; 1 Corinthians 6:18; 10:14; etc.). How are you training yourself to make godly choices? —C. R. B.

## II. Miraculous Intervention
(Exodus 14:21-28)

### A. Israelites Escape (vv. 21, 22)

**21. And Moses stretched out his hand over the sea; and the Lord caused the sea to go back by a strong east wind all that night, and made the sea dry land, and the waters were divided.**

There are two things in Exodus 14:15-20 (not in today's text) that we should note as we move to verse 21. First, verse 16 tells us that Moses is stretching out not just *his hand,* but the "rod" that has been the visible means of God's power throughout the plagues. This rod has been important from the beginning of this deliverance (see Exodus 4:17). Many times the text recounts that Moses stretches out this rod to do signs and miracles (see Exodus 7:19, 20; 8:5, 16, 17; 9:23; 10:13; 17:9-12). However, Moses eventually uses the rod in a way that displeases God (see Numbers 20:11).

We may wonder why God even bothers to use Moses and his rod to get things done. It seems to be a principle that God prefers to work through the human instrument. God usually finds someone to push His plan forward (example: Isaiah 6:8), but sometimes He doesn't (example: Ezekiel 22:30). Yet even when the human instrument is involved, we know that the signs and miracles ultimately come from God.

This is no less true when God uses natural forces to accomplish a task, with the miracle being in the intensity and timing of those forces. For example, consider how God uses the wind in the verse before us. We experience wind almost daily as a natural, nonmiraculous force of nature that God has put in place for the normal functioning of the world. The miraculous element here is in the intensity and duration of the wind as God causes *the sea to go back by a strong east wind all that night* (compare also Exodus 10:13).

The way the text actually reads should cause healthy skepticism as we consider how Hollywood recreates accounts from the Bible. For example, Cecil B. DeMille's 1956 movie *The Ten Commandments* is inaccurate in showing the waters parting almost instantly as Charlton Heston, playing the part of Moses, raises his staff. That's not how it happened. God certainly could have done it that way, but He chose a different procedure.

The second thing to note from Exodus 14:15-20 is that the angel of God causes "the pillar of the cloud" to separate the Egyptian army from the Israelites; the result is "a cloud and darkness" to the Egyptians, but a source of light "by night" to the Israelites. This means that the Israelites can witness what is happening *all that night* while the Egyptians cannot.

**22. And the children of Israel went into the midst of the sea upon the dry ground: and the waters were a wall unto them on their right hand, and on their left.**

The fact that it is still night as *the children of Israel* cross *the sea upon the dry ground* is confirmed by the fact that God does not destroy the Egyptians until "the morning watch" (v. 24, below). Even though it is night, the Israelites have light to see by, as noted previously. Surely they recognize that God is indeed fighting for them (v. 14)! We take for granted that Moses leads the way into

## HOW TO SAY IT

| | |
|---|---|
| Canaan | *Kay*-nun. |
| Corinth | *Kor*-inth. |
| Egyptians | Ee-*jip*-shuns. |
| Etham | *E*-thum. |
| Pharaoh | *Fair*-o or *Fay*-roe. |

the parted waters on *dry ground*; then the Israelites followed as sheep follow their shepherd (Isaiah 63:11).

As a conjecture, we might consider the possibility that God could have formed the walls of water *on their right hand, and on their left* by means of a strong jet stream of air that freezes the water as it piles up. As this happens, the seabed may become frozen mud. This theory does not contradict the fact that the text says *dry ground.* I live in Illinois, and on a cold winter's night I can walk across a field of frozen mud as dry ground since there will be no water on the bottom of my shoes after I cross. My conjecture fits well with the statement that "the depths were congealed in the heart of the sea" (Exodus 15:8).

I realize that this is my imagination at work, but it is plausible. It is also possible that the east wind is not cold and that the wind itself holds up the walls of water on both sides. The problem this theory presents is the great difficulty (if not impossibility) of the Israelites being able to walk through such a strong force of continual wind as they pass between the walls of water.

In any case, it is still a miracle! The mixed emotions of this journey between two walls of water surely include fear, excitement, joy, even helplessness. So the Israelites escape.

*What Do You Think?*

What characteristics of a leader will result in people following that leader? What does this tell us about Christian leadership development?

*Talking Points for Your Discussion*

- Regarding leaders in the church
- Regarding Christians who are leaders in business or government
- "Leaders are born" vs. "leaders are made"

### B. Egyptians Pursue (v. 23)

**23. And the Egyptians pursued, and went in after them to the midst of the sea, even all Pharaoh's horses, his chariots, and his horsemen.**

What makes Pharaoh order his chariots and horsemen into the parted waters, clearly a frightening situation if there ever was one? It is God

Visual for Lesson 12

*Point to this visual as you compare the Red Sea deliverance with our deliverance in Christ.*

fighting for Israel by hardening the hearts of the Egyptians (Exodus 14:4, 8, 17). They are remorseful for having let Israel go (v. 5). God had halted their pursuit temporarily (vv. 19, 20), but now they resume the chase. Hard hearts tend to throw caution to the wind.

### C. God Fights (vv. 24, 25)

**24. And it came to pass, that in the morning watch the LORD looked unto the host of the Egyptians through the pillar of fire and of the cloud, and troubled the host of the Egyptians,**

There are several watches throughout the night, and *the morning watch* is the one that occurs from 2 to 6 a.m. God's divine presence is manifested by *the pillar of fire and of the cloud* as it has been before (Exodus 13:21, 22; 14:19). Ancient cultures often depict deity by a brilliant fire in the midst of clouds. It is in such a manifestation that God is presented as observing the Egyptian army and troubling them.

**25. And took off their chariot wheels, that they drave them heavily: so that the Egyptians said, Let us flee from the face of Israel; for the LORD fighteth for them against the Egyptians.**

Part of the troubling or confusion is accomplished by God's destroying the wheels of the chariots. If the previous conjecture regarding "frozen mud" is correct, it would be nothing for God to thaw the mud so that chariot wheels become mired, with the result that the wheels come off.

The result is panic among the charioteers. Such a result undoubtedly spreads among the rank and file of the Egyptian army, causing great confusion. Even the Egyptians are able to recognize that God is fighting for the Israelites (compare Exodus 14:14; Deuteronomy 1:30; 3:22)! The Egyptians' attempt to turn around and flee from the Israelites, now on the other side of the sea, further adds to the confusion and paralysis.

*What Do You Think?*

What battles has God fought for you? What made you realize that you needed to relinquish control and allow Him to fight that battle?

*Talking Points for Your Discussion*

- Psalms 37:7-9; 44:6, 7; 124:1-5
- Romans 8:35-37
- 2 Corinthians 1:8-11
- 1 John 5:4, 5
- Other

### D. Egyptians Perish (vv. 26-28)

**26. And the LORD said unto Moses, Stretch out thine hand over the sea, that the waters may come again upon the Egyptians, upon their chariots, and upon their horsemen.**

God can, of course, simply speak the word and cause the waters to *come again upon the Egyptians* without any participation by Moses. But the people need to see that Moses is the leader that God has chosen, so God works through him to finish off the pursuers.

**27. And Moses stretched forth his hand over the sea, and the sea returned to his strength when the morning appeared; and the Egyptians fled against it; and the LORD overthrew the Egyptians in the midst of the sea.**

The phrase *when the morning appeared* again confirms that the crossing takes place at night. The Israelites can see their great deliverance unfolding. The doctrinal points of these events are clearly stated several times throughout the story: the Egyptians know (before they die!) the identity of the one true God (Exodus 14:4, 17, 18), and the Israelites acknowledge God with reverent fear and trust in Him and His servant Moses (14:13, 14, 30, 31).

*What Do You Think?*

How does your deliverance by God from past circumstances help you face the next battle?

*Talking Points for Your Discussion*

- In how you view trying circumstances (2 Kings 6:13-17)
- In how you pray (Luke 22:42)
- In how you help others going through difficult times (1 Peter 4:12-19)
- Other

**28. And the waters returned, and covered the chariots, and the horsemen, and all the host of Pharaoh that came into the sea after them; there remained not so much as one of them.**

The fact that the returning waters are deep enough to cover *the chariots, and the horsemen, and all the host of Pharaoh* indicates that the Israelites are not crossing a shallow, marshy lake as some have proposed. Such a theory is disallowed by the fact that the army of Pharaoh at the Red Sea perishes in the manner described here.

Although there may be parts of the army left back in Egypt that did not pursue Israel, the power of Egypt is so weakened that it is no factor in Canaan until the days of the Israelite monarchy, hundreds of years later. The statement *there remained not so much as one of them* acts as a bookend with verse 13: "For the Egyptians whom ye have seen to day, ye shall see them again no more for ever."

### *Power from Above*

The "Arab Spring" of 2011 led to profound changes in North Africa. Uprisings in Egypt and Libya toppled autocratic regimes in those two countries. The rebels and their Western allies used modern "from above" communication technology to coordinate efforts, as messages sent over social media via satellites, etc., brought a new level of sophistication to civil-disobedience movements.

The uprising in Libya saw another "from above" technology used in overthrowing the government: that of air power, as a combination of manned and drone aircraft assisted rebel forces. Such "from above" power proved to be decisive.

The ancient Israelites were the rebels against Pharaoh's entrenched power. That ancient tyrant discovered that he was no match for the power that came against him from above—the power of the one and only God Almighty. Modern technology is nice to have, but its presence also lends itself to a certain danger: the danger of relying on it to the exclusion of the ultimate power from above. Think back to the day before you read this lesson. How much time did you spend in prayer in comparison with the amount of time you spent fiddling with the various high-tech gadgets on which we all rely so much? —C. R. B.

## III. Victorious Resolution

(Exodus 14:29, 30)

### A. Summary of Deliverance (v. 29)

**29. But the children of Israel walked upon dry land in the midst of the sea; and the waters were a wall unto them on their right hand, and on their left.**

This is a repeat of verse 22 with slight variation in verbs and word order. It functions as a conclusion for this section of the story that stretches from verse 21 to verse 29.

*What Do You Think?*

What "Red Sea experience" are you facing right now? What will be God's part and what will be your part in the victory to come?

*Talking Points for Your Discussion*

- Regarding a pending confrontation
- Regarding a financial difficulty
- Regarding a difficult area of ministry
- Other

### B. Evidence of Freedom (v. 30)

**30. Thus the Lord saved Israel that day out of the hand of the Egyptians; and Israel saw the Egyptians dead upon the sea shore.**

This is an epilogue to the story. Israel sees "the salvation of the Lord" (v. 13) as evidenced by *the Egyptians dead upon the sea shore.* The Egyptian charioteers and horsemen are no match for the divine warrior. The "Song of Moses" that follows celebrates this victory over Pharaoh's army (see Exodus 15:1-21). The fact of this deliverance is restated often (see Deuteronomy 11:4; Joshua 2:10; 4:23; 24:6, 7; Judges 11:16; Isaiah 51:10; 63:11-13) and remembered frequently in Israel's hymns (see Psalms 66:6; 77:19, 20; 78:13, 53; 106:7, 9, 22; 114:3, 5; 136:13, 15). The result is that the Israelites fear God and trust not only Him but also Moses (Exodus 14:31, immediately following today's text). Sadly, subsequent events will show how fleeting that fear and trust to be.

## Conclusion

### A. Our Great Salvation

Hebrews 3 compares and contrasts the faithfulness of Moses as a servant of God with the faithfulness of Jesus as the Son of God. While Israel's deliverance from slavery was great, the Christian's salvation from sin is far greater. The apostle Paul uses the exodus event to warn his readers in Corinth by comparing their status in Christ with Israel's baptism unto Moses (1 Corinthians 10:1, 2). Because of the Israelites' subsequent unfaithfulness, they were condemned to die in the wilderness (v. 5). In spite of our baptism into Christ, we may suffer the same condemnation if we prove to be unfaithful (vv. 6-12).

We must show gratitude for our great salvation in Jesus Christ. We do this by obedience to Christ's law of love. We must not be as the generation that left Egypt after witnessing the miracles of the plagues only to express doubt, fear, and sarcasm as the pursuing army approached (Exodus 14:10-12). "Now all these things happened unto them for ensamples: and they are written for our admonition, upon whom the ends of the world are come" (1 Corinthians 10:11).

### B. Prayer

Our Father, we praise You for the great salvation we have in Christ. May we never take Your grace for granted or cheapen it by shallow discipleship. Help us to keep our eyes on the promised eternal life. Till Jesus comes, amen.

### C. Thought to Remember

Expect God's deliverance.

# INVOLVEMENT LEARNING

*Some of the activities below are also found in the helpful student book,* Adult Bible Class.
*Don't forget to download the free reproducible page from www.standardlesson.com to enhance your lesson!*

## Into the Lesson

*Option:* Place in chairs copies of the "Egyptians Fall, Part 2" exercise from the reproducible page, which you can download. Learners can begin working on this as they arrive. (*Alternative:* Distribute this at the end of class as a take-home activity.)

Prepare two small posters, each featuring the word *water.* Affix these to the door frame of your learning area, one poster on each side. As class begins, ask, "Will someone please explain the symbolism of our entrance today?" The symbolism, of course, relates to Israel's passing between the walls of water in today's text.

Say, "Last week's lesson was about a *passing over,* while this week's study is about a *passing through.* This was a real 'sight to see' for the ancient Israelites, and it will be for us as well."

## Into the Word

To continue with the "sight to see" theme, say, "I have something for you to see: signs . . . not miraculous ones, but ones you might see along the way of life. See if you can associate them with an idea or verse from the text." Reveal the signs below in sequence. The signs can be simple words on sheets of paper, but making these appear as road signs will enhance their visual appeal. After revealing a sign, pause for associations with the text; expected responses are noted.

*Dead End*—The Israelites' feeling of being trapped.

*Danger*—The threat from Pharaoh's finest warriors.

*Warning: High Wind*—The strong, all-night wind to move the waters where God wanted them.

*Warning: Severe Tire Damage*—The destruction of Pharaoh's chariots.

*Enter at Your Own Risk*—Pharaoh's sending his army after the Israelites.

*Water Unsafe for Swimming*—The drownings that occurred.

*Exit*—God's deliverance.

*Littering Permitted*—The littering of the shoreline with the dead.

*Scenic Overlook*—Seeing the results of God's intervention.

*One Way*—The path of obedience and trust.

*No U-Turn Allowed*—The futility of the Egyptians' attempted retreat.

As learners respond, offer additional commentary as appropriate.

*Alternative:* If you wish to use small groups, distribute handouts titled *What a Sight to See . . . and Not See!* Have several blank lines below the title. Say, "In Exodus 14:13, God promises a sight to see and a sight never to be seen again. What are those two sights?" *(Answers: deliverance would be seen; pursuing Egyptians would not be seen again.)* Then say, "Read through today's text plus verses 15-20. As you do, make a list of what you would have seen if you had been one of the escaping Israelites."

## Into Life

Say, "The deliverance of the Israelites prompted praise in song (Exodus 15, not in today's text). What are some of your favorite songs or hymns that express your praise in Jesus' deliverance from sin?" Encourage a time of unstructured sharing.

*Alternative:* Invite one of your musically talented learners to lead the class in a song, hymn, or chorus that speaks of the joy of our salvation in Christ (examples: "There Is Power in the Blood," "Redeemed," and "Shout to the North.")

Say, "Immediately following the events in today's text, Moses led the Israelites in a song of joyous praise (Exodus 15:1-18). Our salvation in Jesus should always elicit this kind of praise." Distribute copies of the "A Time to Sing" activity from the reproducible page for learners to use in their devotional times in the week ahead.

# Beginning of the Tabernacle

**Devotional Reading:** Hebrews 9:11-15
**Background Scripture:** Exodus 35–40

## Exodus 40:16-30, 34, 38

**16 Thus did Moses: according to all that the Lord commanded him, so did he.**

**17 And it came to pass in the first month in the second year, on the first day of the month, that the tabernacle was reared up.**

**18 And Moses reared up the tabernacle, and fastened his sockets, and set up the boards thereof, and put in the bars thereof, and reared up his pillars.**

**19 And he spread abroad the tent over the tabernacle, and put the covering of the tent above upon it; as the Lord commanded Moses.**

**20 And he took and put the testimony into the ark, and set the staves on the ark, and put the mercy seat above upon the ark:**

**21 And he brought the ark into the tabernacle, and set up the vail of the covering, and covered the ark of the testimony; as the Lord commanded Moses.**

**22 And he put the table in the tent of the congregation, upon the side of the tabernacle northward, without the vail.**

**23 And he set the bread in order upon it before the Lord; as the Lord had commanded Moses.**

**24 And he put the candlestick in the tent of the congregation, over against the table, on the side of the tabernacle southward.**

**25 And he lighted the lamps before the Lord; as the Lord commanded Moses.**

**26 And he put the golden altar in the tent of the congregation before the vail:**

**27 And he burnt sweet incense thereon; as the Lord commanded Moses.**

**28 And he set up the hanging at the door of the tabernacle.**

**29 And he put the altar of burnt offering by the door of the tabernacle of the tent of the congregation, and offered upon it the burnt offering and the meat offering; as the Lord commanded Moses.**

**30 And he set the laver between the tent of the congregation and the altar, and put water there, to wash withal.**

. . . . . . . . . . . . . . . . . . . . . . . . . . .

**34 Then a cloud covered the tent of the congregation, and the glory of the Lord filled the tabernacle.**

. . . . . . . . . . . . . . . . . . . . . . . . . . .

**38 For the cloud of the Lord was upon the tabernacle by day, and fire was on it by night, in the sight of all the house of Israel, throughout all their journeys.**

## Key Verse

*The cloud of the Lord was upon the tabernacle by day, and fire was on it by night, in the sight of all the house of Israel, throughout all their journeys.* **—Exodus 40:38**

# First Things

## Unit 3: First Freedom

Lessons 10–13

## Lesson Aims

After participating in this lesson, each student will be able to:

1. Match the tabernacle's furnishings with their functions.

2. Compare and contrast God's presence in the tabernacle with His presence in the temple in Jerusalem, in Jesus, in the church, and in the individual Christian.

3. Demonstrate God's presence in his or her life in a concrete way in the week ahead.

## Lesson Outline

Introduction
- A. Building My Tabernacle
- B. Lesson Background

I. Constructing the Tabernacle (Exodus 40: 16-19)
- A. Obedience of Moses (v. 16)
  - *Doing It God's Way*
- B. Date of Completion (v. 17)
- C. Structure of the Sanctuary (vv. 18, 19)

II. Furnishing the Tabernacle (Exodus 40: 20-30)
- A. The Holy of Holies (vv. 20, 21)
- B. The Tent of Meeting (vv. 22-28)
- C. The Courtyard (vv. 29, 30)
  - *Building the Building and the Body*

III. Presence at the Tabernacle (Exodus 40: 34, 38)
- A. Cloud and Glory (v. 34)
- B. Cloud and Fire (v. 38)

Conclusion
- A. Living in God's Presence
- B. Prayer
- C. Thought to Remember

## Introduction

### A. Building My Tabernacle

One of the great experiences in my childhood was the opportunity to construct a model tabernacle in Vacation Bible School, using a kit from Standard Publishing. It was the mid-1950s, and I was in the fifth grade. My VBS group was taught by the preacher, and he led us in a weeklong Bible study (mostly from Exodus 25–40) of the tabernacle and its furnishings. I remember using gold, silver, and copper paint during craft time to cover the posts and bases of our model.

I felt like I was building something special, so I was aggravated when my friend Doug was sloppy with the paint. It seemed that he couldn't have cared less about how the model tabernacle looked. I was disappointed at the end result because "it just wasn't right." But when we had our closing program in the evening, I was surprised when I saw our project displayed. It was perfect! Only later did I learn that our teacher had busied himself that afternoon repainting and touching up. Of course, we boys took the credit in front of our parents and the congregation, but secretly we knew who had made the model tabernacle look so good.

I don't remember much about our lessons that week, but I still remember the experience of building the tabernacle. It made me think more deeply about God's presence. Our lesson today has something to teach us in that regard.

### B. Lesson Background

Ancient Israel's tabernacle can be thought of as a portable temple. Exodus 40 is a conclusion to all the instructions regarding the tabernacle proper (Exodus 25–31) and how it was built (Exodus 35–39). We may call these multichapter sections "the two narratives of the tabernacle." Exodus 40:1-11 parallels the *in*struction narrative of Exodus 25–31, while Exodus 40:16-33 parallels the *con*struction narrative of Exodus 35–39. Exodus 40:12-15 is not exactly a parallel; it deals with Aaron (Moses' brother) and his sons, about whom details are given in Exodus 28, 29 and Leviticus 8:1-13.

The golden calf story of Exodus 32–34 has been placed between the two narratives of the tabernacle. Knowing the reason for this deliberate placement helps us appreciate more fully the tabernacle's purpose.

Moses' delay on the mountain (Exodus 32:1) resulted in the Israelites becoming anxious, so they expressed to Aaron a desire to have a visible representation of deity ("gods"). Previously, the people had been very afraid even to listen to God lest they die, and they had implored Moses to intercede (see Exodus 20:18-20; Deuteronomy 5:23-27). What the people demanded of Aaron was a material, visible entity to substitute for Moses' intercession between them and the presence of the invisible God. Exodus 32–34 therefore represents false worship as God was, in effect, put back into nature in the form of a calf. By contrast, the tabernacle and its furnishings represented true worship where God's presence was rightly displayed.

## I. Constructing the Tabernacle

(Exodus 40:16-19)

### A. Obedience of Moses (v. 16)

**16. Thus did Moses: according to all that the Lord commanded him, so did he.**

At the beginning of the instructions, God had said to Moses, "let them make me a sanctuary; that I may dwell among them. According to all that I shew thee, after the pattern of the tabernacle, and the pattern of all the instruments thereof, even so shall ye make it" (Exodus 25:8, 9). Moses is to ensure that the tabernacle furnishings are made according to the instructions given to him on Mount Sinai (25:40). Moses also is to erect the tabernacle according to God's specifications (26:30). The work itself is done primarily by many skilled workers (see 31:1-11; 35:4–38:23), but Moses is in charge of making sure that everything is done right.

By the time we reach the verse before us, the phrase *all that the Lord commanded him, so did he* (or a variation of it) has been repeated numerous times with regard to the tabernacle's construction. It will be repeated several more times between here and the end of the book. Moses is meticulous in his obedience.

*What Do You Think?*

What are some benefits of complete obedience to God? What may be the cost of such obedience?

*Talking Points for Your Discussion*

- Matthew 19:27-29
- John 13:14-17
- Acts 5:27-29, 40, 41
- James 1:25
- Other

### *Doing It God's Way*

Most of us have a stubborn streak. We like to do things a certain way, and we also prefer that others do things the way we want them done. Frank Sinatra's famous song "My Way" echoes this kind of stubborn individualism.

Sometimes the *my way* approach involves whole communities. For example, residents of the small village of Town Line, New York, voted in 1861 to secede from the Union, reportedly on a vote of 85 to 40. The village didn't officially end its break with the Union until a new vote was taken on January 24, 1946!

"Doing it my way" may mean having blinders on regarding the wisdom of a different course of action. It may mean ignoring the likely consequences of stubbornly pushing ahead when circumstances suggest that we would be wise to reconsider our position. If we're not careful, our stubbornness may lead us into the trap of convincing ourselves that our way "must be" God's way. That seems to have been the problem of Jesus' opponents during His ministry on earth. Do we ever repeat this error? —C. R. B.

## HOW TO SAY IT

| | |
|---|---|
| acacia | uh-*kay*-shuh. |
| Gabriel | *Gay*-bree-ul. |
| Herod | *Hair*-ud. |
| omnipresence | *ahm*-nih-***prez***-ence. |
| Pentecost | *Pent*-ih-kost. |
| shittim | shih-*teem*. |
| tabernacle | ***tah***-burr-*nah*-kul. |
| Titus Flavius | *Ty*-tus *Flay*-vee-us. |
| Zacharias | Zack-uh-*rye*-us. |

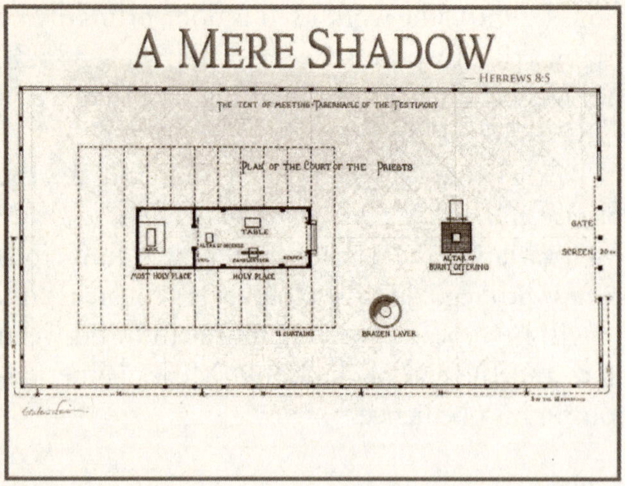


Visual for Lesson 13. *Point to this visual as you discuss why the tabernacle was "the example and shadow of heavenly things" (Hebrews 8:5).*

### B. Date of Completion (v. 17)

**17. And it came to pass in the first month in the second year, on the first day of the month, that the tabernacle was reared up.**

*The second year* is a reference to the beginning of the exodus from Egypt. The Israelites had arrived in the wilderness of Sinai "in the third month . . . the same day" after their departure (Exodus 19:1). Therefore, the people have been in this area for 10 months by the time the tabernacle is finished. The raising of the tabernacle on the one-year anniversary of the exodus reinforces the idea that the Israelites are a distinct people. What a New Year's Day!

### C. Structure of the Sanctuary (vv. 18, 19)

**18. And Moses reared up the tabernacle, and fastened his sockets, and set up the boards thereof, and put in the bars thereof, and reared up his pillars.**

The statement *Moses reared up the tabernacle* refers to the tabernacle proper—that is, the walls (see Exodus 26:15-30; 36:20-34). For each item listed in the verse before us, we will note references both to the instructions about it (in Exodus 25–31) and to its construction (in Exodus 35–39).

The foundation of the tabernacle consists of 100 *sockets.* There are 40 for the north and south walls each (Exodus 26:18-21). There are 14 for the west (back) side with 2 additional corner sockets to make a total of 16 there (26:22-25). The remaining 4 are used for the pillars that are discussed below.

Placed in the sockets are 48 gold-covered *boards* made of shittim (acacia) wood. Each measures 10 cubits high by 1½ cubits wide (Exodus 26:16; 36:21). There are 20 boards on the north (26:20; 36:25), 20 on the south (26:18; 36:23), 6 on the west (26:22; 36:27), and 2 corner ones (26:23; 36:28).

There are four gold-covered *bars* to hold the boards in place. The middle bar apparently goes through the boards themselves for extra stability. Separating the most holy place (the holy of holies) from the holy place is a veil that hangs on four gold-covered *pillars* (26:31-35; 36:35, 36). We note five more pillars used for the entrance to the tabernacle (26:36, 37; 36:37, 38).

**19. And he spread abroad the tent over the tabernacle, and put the covering of the tent above upon it; as the LORD commanded Moses.**

*The tent over the tabernacle* and *the covering of the tent* consist of numerous curtains (Exodus 26:7-14; 36:14-19). These are made from layers of cloth and skin. There are many artists' sketches of what these coverings may have looked like.

## II. Furnishing the Tabernacle

(EXODUS 40:20-30)

### A. The Holy of Holies (vv. 20, 21)

**20. And he took and put the testimony into the ark, and set the staves on the ark, and put the mercy seat above upon the ark.**

The ark of the testimony (Exodus 25:10-22; 37:1-9) is the focal point of the tabernacle because it is the exact location for God's presence and revelation for Moses and the high priest. The special feature of the ark's covering is two cherubims molded of pure gold (25:17-22; 37:1-8).

The cherubims have wings that meet each other, and their faces look down on *the mercy seat,* the place where God will meet with Moses (Exodus 25:22; compare Numbers 7:89). The Israelites will come to envision the mercy seat to be God's "footstool," the place of His feet, while His throne is in Heaven itself (see 1 Chronicles 28:2; Psalm 99:5; 132:7; Lamentations 2:1). God establishes the sprinkling of blood on the mercy seat for forgiveness of sins (Leviticus 16:14-16). This foreshadows what Christ does for us (Hebrews 9; 1 Peter 1:2).

*The testimony* that is put into the ark refers to the stone tablets of the Ten Commandments. Other things will be put in later (Exodus 16:33, 34; Numbers 17:10, 11; compare Hebrews 9:4). *The staves* are used for carrying the ark since to touch the ark itself is to invite death (Exodus 37:4, 5; 25:14-16; 1 Chronicles 13:9, 10).

**21. And he brought the ark into the tabernacle, and set up the vail of the covering, and covered the ark of the testimony; as the LORD commanded Moses.**

The beautifully crafted *vail of the covering* is hung on four wooden pillars that are overlaid with gold and placed in silver sockets (Exodus 26:31-35; 36:35, 36); this vail (or veil) is designed to conceal *the ark of the testimony* (later known more commonly as "the ark of the covenant" per Numbers 10:33; etc.) from the priests. Only once a year will the high priest be allowed to enter into the holy of holies (Leviticus 16). Jesus' death and atonement for our sins has enabled every believer to enter into God's presence today; the veil has been torn asunder (see Matthew 27:51; Mark 15:38; Hebrews 9:11-14; 10:19-25; and 1 Peter 3:18).

*What Do You Think?*

Thinking of the veil or curtain that Christ tore down in Mark 15:38, how can we ensure that we do not put up veils that may hinder relationships (ours or others') with God?

*Talking Points for Your Discussion*

- Veils of wrong priorities
- Veils of traditions
- Veils of legalism
- Other

### B. The Tent of Meeting (vv. 22-28)

**22, 23. And he put the table in the tent of the congregation, upon the side of the tabernacle northward, without the vail. And he set the bread in order upon it before the LORD; as the LORD had commanded Moses.**

*The table in the tent of the congregation,* located on the north side of the holy place (Exodus 25:23-30; 37:10-16), is primarily for the "shewbread." This consists of 12 cakes made of "fine flour," each cake representing a tribe (Leviticus 24:5-7). That is the reference of *set the bread in order.*

The bread represents God's provision in the wilderness. It is to be replaced every Sabbath with fresh bread (Leviticus 24:8). Only priests are allowed eat this bread and only in the holy place (Leviticus 24:9; see an exception in 1 Samuel 21:4; compare Matthew 12:3, 4). The table also includes utensils for wine and drink offerings (Exodus 37:16).

**24, 25. And he put the candlestick in the tent of the congregation, over against the table, on the side of the tabernacle southward. And he lighted the lamps before the LORD; as the LORD commanded Moses.**

*The candlestick* is made from a solid piece of gold; it is hammered out so that the candlestick rises from a base to form a middle stem with three branches on each side, modeled as a flowering almond tree (Exodus 25:31-36; 37:17-24). Thus, there are seven oil-filled bowls that provide light in the tabernacle (25:37; 27:20, 21).

The candlestick is probably about three and a half feet tall. (There is a depiction of it carved into the Arch of Triumph in Rome; the carving depicts the successful conclusion of the siege of Jerusalem by Titus Flavius in AD 70.) The candlestick is located on the south side, opposite the table of the shewbread.

*What Do You Think?*

What do you need to do to make sure that Christ continues to be the candlestick or lamp that lights your way?

*Talking Points for Your Discussion*

- Psalm 119:105
- 1 John 1:7
- Revelation 1:12, 13

**26, 27. And he put the golden altar in the tent of the congregation before the vail: and he burnt sweet incense thereon; as the LORD commanded Moses.**

*The golden altar* is for burning incense; it is not to be used for burnt offerings (Exodus 30:1-10; compare 37:25-28). It is placed *before the vail,* behind which stands the ark of the covenant. The aroma of *sweet incense* wafts into the holy of holies to represent the prayers of the people rising into God's presence (see Exodus 30:34; compare Psalm 141:2; Revelation 5:8). Once per year, the high priest anoints the horns of this altar with blood for the atonement of the people (Exodus 30:10; Leviticus 16:18). This altar is part of the setting of Gabriel's appearance to Zacharias in Luke 1.

**28. And he set up the hanging at the door of the tabernacle.**

The curtain *at the door of the tabernacle* is similar in construction to the inner veil (Exodus 26:36; 36:37). This curtain hangs on five golden pillars. But unlike the four pillars for the veil set in silver sockets, the sockets for this entrance curtain are covered with brass (26:37; 36:38). This is probably because they can be seen from outside and so are considered part of the brass items in the courtyard (38:2-6; etc.).

*What Do You Think?*

What does the quality and particularity of the tabernacle furnishings have to say about how we should furnish church buildings, if anything?

*Talking Points for Your Discussion*

- Cost vs. value
- "'The best' is the enemy of 'good enough'"
- Matthew 26:8-13

### C. The Courtyard (vv. 29, 30)

**29. And he put the altar of burnt offering by the door of the tabernacle of the tent of the congregation, and offered upon it the burnt offering and the meat offering; as the LORD commanded Moses.**

*The altar of burnt offering* is sometimes called "the brasen altar" (Exodus 38:30; 39:39; etc.). The sacrifices to be placed on it are described in Leviticus 1:1–7:38.

The horns of this altar (Exodus 27:2; 38:2) are sacred, and sinners can flee to them to avoid punishment. Others will flee to these horns in hopes of forgiveness or compassion from earthly enemies (see 1 Kings 1:50-53; 2:28-34). This altar foreshadows Christ, who is our perfect sacrifice and the altar for our redemption (see Hebrews 9:11-15).

**30. And he set the laver between the tent of the congregation and the altar, and put water there, to wash withal.**

*The laver* is a large bowl with a stand, both of brass (Exodus 30:17-21). These are made from "the lookingglasses of the women assembling . . . at the door of the tabernacle of the congregation" (38:8). These brass mirrors, highly polished and beautiful, were probably procured from the Egyptians during the exodus (12:35, 36).

The priests have to be "clean" each time they enter the tabernacle or offer sacrifices, so this laver is for washing in that regard. The penalty for priests not washing their feet and hands is death (Exodus 30:20, 21)! So the altar and laver go together (compare Ephesians 5:26; Titus 3:5).

### *Building the Building and the Body*

Church building programs can be exciting experiences. Ideally, the process will unite the congregation in joyfully completing the task. But some congregations find the process to be a source of strife. In one church, the men on the board —good businessmen with good hearts—made fiscally responsible decisions on some aesthetic matters that aroused the ire of the artistically minded women of the church. In another church, the battle over the color of the carpet in the women's lounge caused several families to leave!

The source of such conflicts may be as simple as was stated by one combatant: "If this church is being built with my money, then I'm going to have a say in how it is built!" Danger looms when such a cantankerous spirit presents itself, and the damage can be significant.

Moses had lots of challenges in dealing with a fickle people, but dealing with a building committee was not one of them. God himself decided the sizes, shapes, colors, and materials of the tabernacle's architecture and furnishings. As for the building fund, the Egyptians had made a major contribution! Whether we are building a church building or the body of Christ, the continuous challenge is to keep our focus on what the divine architect, the master builder, would have us do. That's really the only way to keep our personal preferences in check. —C. R. B.

## III. Presence at the Tabernacle

(Exodus 40:34, 38)

### A. Cloud and Glory (v. 34)

**34. Then a cloud covered the tent of the congregation, and the glory of the Lord filled the tabernacle.**

Although God is everywhere, He chooses to dwell among His people in a tent in a special way. No tent or temple can contain the Creator God, of course (Acts 17:24). But the purpose of the tabernacle is to have a symbol of God's presence. So after Moses sets up the tabernacle and consecrates it with oil, God manifests himself in a cloud that envelopes the tent, and thus His glory fills the tabernacle. God's divine presence is in the midst of His people, and His people can see it!

The parallel between this scene and the cloud and glory on Mount Sinai (Exodus 24:15-18) should encourage the people. God now moves the manifestation of His presence from Sinai to be with them on their journey (compare 13:21, 22; 14:19, 24; 16:10; 33:9, 10, 22; 34:5). This idea will develop more fully as time passes.

### B. Cloud and Fire (v. 38)

**38. For the cloud of the Lord was upon the tabernacle by day, and fire was on it by night, in the sight of all the house of Israel, throughout all their journeys.**

In the fire and cloud hovering over the tabernacle, the Israelites have a visible, awe-inspiring symbol of God's presence in their midst. No one can deny it. All they can do is follow it. God is on a journey with His people and His people with Him (see Numbers 9:15-23; 10:11-28).

*What Do You Think?*

What "visual aids" have you found to be helpful reminders that Jesus is leading you on your journey?

*Talking Points for Your Discussion*

- Artwork displayed year round in your home
- Seasonal displays in your home
- The elements of the Lord's Supper
- Other

## Conclusion

### A. Living in God's Presence

Sin in the Garden of Eden resulted in humanity's losing the privilege of living in God's presence. But God has acted to reverse that situation. Freed from Egyptian bondage, Israel had God's presence in her midst by means of the tabernacle. Instead of cherubims turning away God's children by means of a sharp sword to guard the way to the tree of life (Genesis 3:24), the Israelites had images of cherubims marking the place of God's presence. Perhaps the candlestick stood for the tree of life as it illuminated the holy place.

The manifestation of God's presence was experienced anew when Solomon dedicated the temple (see 1 Kings 8:1–9:9; 2 Chronicles 7). That temple was destroyed in 586 BC because of sin. Rebuilt by the returned exiles, the temple was later enhanced by Herod the Great. Standing in its courts, Jesus declared himself to be the true temple (John 2:19-21; compare Mark 14:58). The apostle John declared "the Word was made flesh, and dwelt [literally, "tabernacled"] among us, (and we beheld his glory, the glory as of the only begotten of the Father,) full of grace and truth" (John 1:14). That was Jesus.

God made His presence known again on the Day of Pentecost. The result was the new temple described in 2 Corinthians 6:16 (see also 1 Corinthians 3:16, 17; Ephesians 2:19-22). Christ is the eternal high priest and the perfect sacrifice in an everlasting tabernacle (Hebrews 8:1–10:18). Today all Christians have access to the most holy place (Hebrews 10:19-22). In the new Jerusalem there will be no temple, for "the Lord God Almighty and the Lamb are the temple of it" (Revelation 21:22). Our future is to live in God's immediate presence forever!

### B. Prayer

Our Father, help us realize Your presence as we worship. May we ever see our body of believers as Your dwelling place. In Jesus' name, amen.

### C. Thought To Remember

Recognize and value God's presence in your life.

# INVOLVEMENT LEARNING

*Some of the activities below are also found in the helpful student book,* Adult Bible Class.
*Don't forget to download the free reproducible page from www.standardlesson.com to enhance your lesson!*

## Into the Lesson

Put the word *GOD* in bold lettering on eight or so index cards. Affix these cards randomly and conspicuously around your classroom; if your learning space has a window, be sure to put one on it (to represent His presence "out there" as well as "in here"). Save one to affix to yourself, ideally inside a coat or even lapel, to represent God's presence within the Christian.

As class begins, ask, "What are we talking about when we speak of God's omnipresence?" *(Expected response: "God is present everywhere.")* Indicate that your signs are a feeble way to represent God's presence at all times in all places. Point to the label you have put on yourself and say, "God lives especially within those who are committed to His will."

Note that today's study from Exodus 40 is a story of God's manifested presence in a special place and for a special time: the tabernacle of the not-yet-settled nation of Israel.

## Into the Word

Distribute copies of the matching quiz below as a pretest. Say, "With Bibles closed, see if you can match each numbered item with its function for the tabernacle. When you finish, we'll go over the results as a class."

***Items:*** 1. altar of burnt offerings; 2. ark; 3. boards; 4. candlestick; 5. golden altar; 6. laver; 7. staves; 8. table; 9. vail (or veil). ***Functions:*** A. for carrying the ark of the testimony; B. for ceremonial washing of hands and feet; C. for sacrifices; D. for the framework of the tabernacle; E. for separating the holy place from the most holy place; F. to burn incense; G. to hold lamps; H. to hold the bread; I. to hold the testimony and serve as a base for the mercy seat. *Answers: 1-C (v. 29); 2-I (v. 20); 3-D (v. 18); 4-G (vv. 24, 25); 5-F (vv. 26, 27); 6-B (v. 30); 7-A (v. 20); 8-H (vv. 22, 23); 9-E (vv. 21, 22, 26).*

Before going over the results, have three learners alternate reading the verses of Exodus 40:16-30 of today's text aloud (do not read verses 34 and 38 yet), then check responses. Lead your learners on an in-depth study of the temple furnishings and their functions by examining fuller explanations in the earlier chapters of Exodus (see the commentary for the cross-references). This will lay the foundation for discussing the climactic events of verses 34 and 38.

Read Exodus 40:34, 38 aloud. Compare and contrast the description of God's presence in these two verses with those of Exodus 19:16-20; 24:15-18; 1 Kings 8:1–9:9; 2 Chronicles 7; Acts 2:1-4; and/or Hebrews 12:18-24.

## Into Life

*Option 1:* Distribute copies of the "'On the Go' Worship" activity from the reproducible page, which you can download. Have learners work on this in pairs or small groups. Stress that the questions need not all be dealt with nor need they be addressed in the sequence listed; learners are free to focus on only one or two questions that they find to be particularly convicting.

*Option 2:* Distribute copies of the "As the Lord Commanded" activity from the reproducible page; have learners work on this in pairs. Stress that this is not an exercise in "patting ourselves on the back" (see Luke 17:10). Rather, the idea is to remind us that Moses is a good model to emulate.

*Option 3:* Distribute peel-and-stick labels, and ask each learner to write *Feet on the Concrete* on his or hers. Say, "Take this home and post it where you will see it frequently in the week ahead. Each time you see it, let it remind you of this basic truth: 'God's presence is a concrete truth; that's where I stand; that's where I walk.' Let this truth encourage you to decide, 'I want to demonstrate my awareness of His presence in all that I do—and don't do—this week.'"